And Other True Stories

Tom Watson

with illustrations by Rose Watson

LONGFELLOW
COMMUNICATIONS

Copyright © 2026 by Tom Watson

All rights reserved.

No part of this publication may be reproduced, distributed, or transmitted in any form or by any means, including photocopying, recording, or other electronic or mechanical methods, without the prior written permission of the publisher, except as permitted by U.S. copyright law. For permission requests, contact Longfellow Communications at hello@longfellowcomms.com.

For privacy reasons, some names, locations, and dates may have been changed.

Library of Congress Cataloging-in-Publication Data
Name: Watson, Tom, March 2026
Title: Your Turn / by Tom Watson. — 1st ed.
ISBN 979-8-218-89522-8
Description: Your Turn: And Other True Stories
Identifiers: LCCN 2025927660
Subjects:
BIOGRAPHY & AUTOBIOGRAPHY / Memoirs
BUSINESS & ECONOMICS / Entrepreneurship
HUMOR / General

Illustrations by Rose Watson
Book cover by Meghan Lambert

Published in Portland, Maine
First edition, 2026

For Rose, Audrey and Sam

Love, Dad

THIS BOOK'S FOR YOU

This book is written for people who've failed multiple times, and yet see that failure is not a permanent condition.

It's also written for:

> People who like to laugh and can laugh at themselves.
> People who have learned from their failures.
> The persistent.
> The resilient.
> The risk takers.
> People who understand the only constant in life is change.
> People who jump without knowing how deep or wide the chasm is below.
> People who struggle with depression and anxiety. Or know folks who do.
> People who have gone through trauma and see it as an opportunity to grow.

Tom Watson
Portland, Maine
February 15, 2025

CONTENTS

WHITE COATS 15

TRIP BEGINS WITH A KISS 37

BREAKER ONE-NINE, YOU COPY? 43

BRIGHT LIGHTS 73

YOU GOT YOUR EARS ON? 89

A CALAMITOUS BLOW 109

SPIRALING UP 127

THE ARENA 139

STINK PIPE GLADIATORS 159

MASTERS OF NOTHING 175

RATS AND WORMS 197

FROM BRICKLAYERS TO MAN BUNS 221

THAT GUY STOLE MY BIKE 253

BARF BAG 281

LIFE IS OUT THERE 303

NOBODY MOVE AND NOBODY GETS HURT 331

YOUR TURN 347

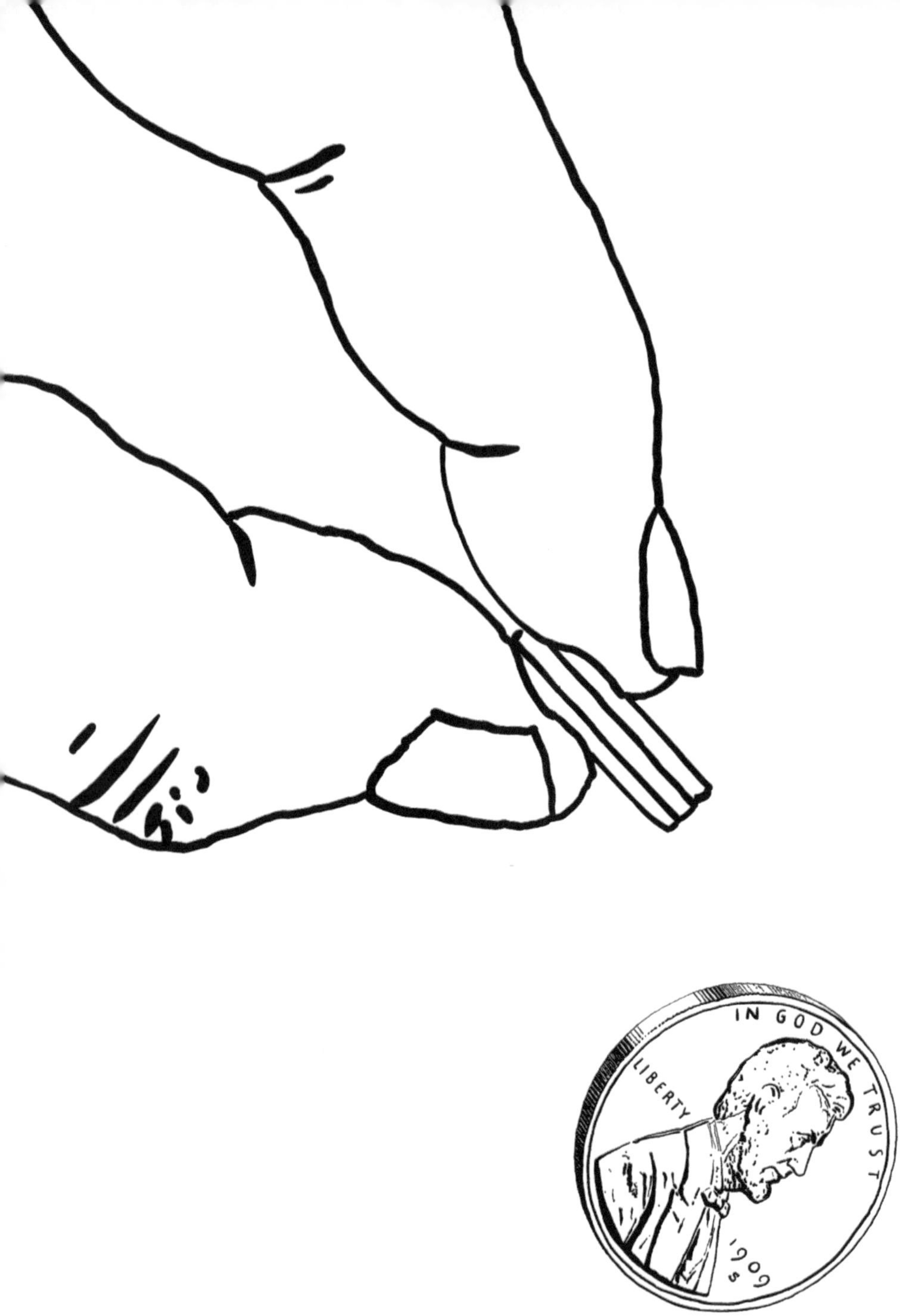
IN GOD WE TRUST
LIBERTY
1909
S

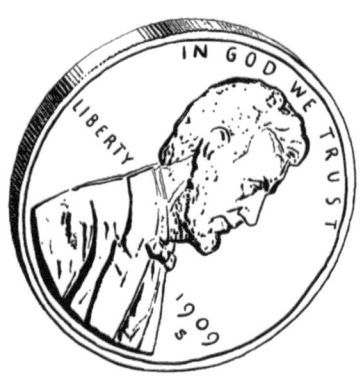

POOR AS CHURCH MICE

My dad, who's been my business partner the last thirty years, refers to us growing up in Massachusetts as "poor as church mice." I don't remember feeling that way.

Didn't feel rich. But didn't feel poor.

First time we went skiing, we went to a small hill one town over, the whole family, my brother seven, me five, my sister three. My dad wouldn't buy the tickets to allow us to use the rope-tow to get up the hill. Instead, we climbed up the hill with our skis on, then skied down. We maybe climbed a quarter-up the hill each time and skied down again and again. We had a blast.

His frugality became embedded in me. In the first building he and I bought together—204 Spring Street in Portland, Maine—we put our sometimes office on an old wooden desk in what became my basement apartment. My mom kept the books along with my dad, the accountant; I did the renovations, maintenance, and leasing. On the desk sat a landline and answering machine.

SUCCEED OR FAIL

When I was a kid, my dad showed me how to paint. In typical style, he explained it fairly quickly, then left me to myself. He'd given me the basics: this is the paint (oil-based), this is the brush, this is how you dip it in the bucket. Wipe some off on the edge. Hold the brush at an angle when you paint the mullion. Drag the brush along until the paint runs out, repeat.

My dad knew I'd make mistakes like get paint on the glass and all over myself. He felt good about this. His thinking then as now is that certain people learn from their mistakes and get better as a result. He saw me as one of those people.

In our home in Acton, Massachusetts, we had a small dining room off the kitchen with a window that looked to the front yard and Arlington Street. The window contained forty-eight panes: eight long, six tall. When I was eleven, I painted the mullions of those twenty-four panes (ninety-six sides), and half-way through I'd become proficient. I loved the work. Tangible work.

The wet paint went on the mullions shiny, and the drab finish disappeared one brush stroke at a time. Suddenly the panes and frames were a brilliant forest green, gleaming like I'd never seen before. I looked at it and thought, I did that. I made it new.

A few years later, when my dad got comfortable with me running up and down a ladder, and moving the ladder from one spot to another, he asked me to paint the outside of the house. The whole house. I think I was fifteen. Same color—a glossy deep brown. It took me a week. Again, I loved it. Most of the work I'd done to date—schoolwork, homework, writing, reading, calculating—didn't have three dimensions. And nobody looked at it other than my teacher briefly to grade it. The sun didn't shine off three plus two equals five. And I couldn't touch it. But the side of our house, newly painted and shining glossy brown—if you wanted to, once it dried you could touch it, even lean against it. The house looked great.

A CONCERNING STORY

ED Provider Notes
Dr. L.
16:03 EST
12/27/21

Patient has a concerning story of transient vision loss.

Out of concern of the symptoms above as well as special concern for the neck pain, transient vision loss, CTA of the head neck chest ordered to look for cervical arterial dissection. Scan ultimately revealed a left artery dissection with concern of subsequent brain infarct and partial occlusion of one of the vertebral arteries. Neurology immediately consulted who came down to visit the patient and provide formal recommendations for management. Patient signed out. Patient very pleasant, no neurological deficits appreciated. Patient resting comfortably.

SIGNED OUT

G. DO

MDM (ED Course and Disposition)

6:42 pm

12/27/2021

Received this patient during sign out. Discussed with neurology. Patient is stable for discharge. He was to be started on Epixaban* 5 mg daily. Plan to follow-up in stroke clinic with Dr. G. Patient should have a repeat CTA in 3 months, this has been ordered and should be followed up with Dr. G. for results.

*blood thinner

VERY LETHARGIC

PFD EMS Patient Care Report
Incident Date: 12/28/2021
15:29:00

On scene, MC4 met E11 crew.

Family reports that patient had been seen at Maine Medical Center yesterday for dizziness. He had been diagnosed with cervical artery dissection. He had been started on Eliquis and discharged. Right before EMS was called, patient suddenly became very lethargic. Reported dizziness. MC4 E11 was dispatched to 13 Birchwood Lane for an adult male who had passed out, conscious now. An MC4 responder is familiar with patient as he transported him yesterday.

ADMISSION

December 28, 2021

Allergies:	Patient has no known allergies
Surgical history:	Knee surgery
Family history:	No known history of bleeding or clotting disorders
Social history:	Married to Judith
	Stanford grad
	Re management, buys apartment buildings, largest in Portland
	3 kids
	Sam in middle school
	Audrey USF
	Rose UCLA
	Running
	Biking
	Tends to overdo it
Diet:	Tends to eat off his kids' leftovers
	Aware he needs to eat more fruits and vegetables
Review of systems:	Unable to obtain due to altered level of consciousness

HOSPITAL STAY

December 30, 2021

From: Maine Medical Hospital Neurology Progress Note

Day: 3

Assessment

Thomas E. Watson is a 59-year-old right-handed man w/hx of HTN and recent R PCA stroke 2/2 L vertebral artery dissection who presented with profound vertigo, N/V, and dysarthria, somnolence, L INO, L facial droop, and L-sided ataxia. CTA revealed top of the basilar thrombus, presumably from his dissection. He underwent successful mechanical thrombectomy of the L PCA and L superior cerebellar artery with intra-arterial TPA. He had no focal deficits on 12/29.

EXTENDED STAY

From: Maine Medical Hospital Neurology Progress Note

Day: 4

Assessment

Presenting for ischemic stroke secondary to cerebrovascular dissection s/p right femoral arteriotomy for thrombectomy and intra-tPA administration 12/28. Started on heparin gtt and converted to apixaban for systemic anticoagulation. Patient noted 'pop' 12/29 with right femoral pain, not radiating. Palpable lump without superficial ecchymosis demonstrating partially thrombosed pseudoaneurysm on 12/31 ultrasound without evidence of fistula vascular compromise.

Reviewed imaging with Interventional Radiology and noted that the dome of the pseudoaneurysm has already thrombosed with neck residual—not a candidate for thrombin injection. Encourage compression as able. Grossly stable H/H 12/31. Low threshold to repeat US if worsened or changing pain, lower extremity selling or color change.

Follow up with Dr. S. in 2-3 weeks, patient advised to call the office if pain worsening or lump progressive in size.

SOCIAL HISTORY

Dr. F.
Mass General Brigham
3/3/2022

Married.
He works in real estate management.
He has 3 kids.
He used to drink 6 ounces of bourbon and 15 ounces of wine nightly.
He is now drinking 8 ounces of red wine nightly.
He is not a smoker.
He has smoked marijuana.
He does follow a healthy diet.
He used to run and bike.

PERSISTENT ABNORMALITIES

Dr. F., Neurologist
Mass General Brigham
Encounter Date: 3/3/2022

On 2/7/2022, he presented again to the Emergency Department with sudden dizziness while eating breakfast, worsening upon standing, gait instability and having to hold onto things while walking, nausea and pain behind the left ear and left neck. A CTA of the head and neck showed persistent abnormalities.

TOES AND FINGERS

If you're being admitted to the hospital via the emergency room on a gurney pushed by paramedics and you don't know that you are, this is not a good place for you to be.

I don't remember being admitted.

I don't remember answering questions whenever I answered them.

The smart, young vascular brain surgeon and his team saved my life, and my limbs, and most of my brain.

I slept for a few days until they woke me to see if my toes and fingers worked.

They did.

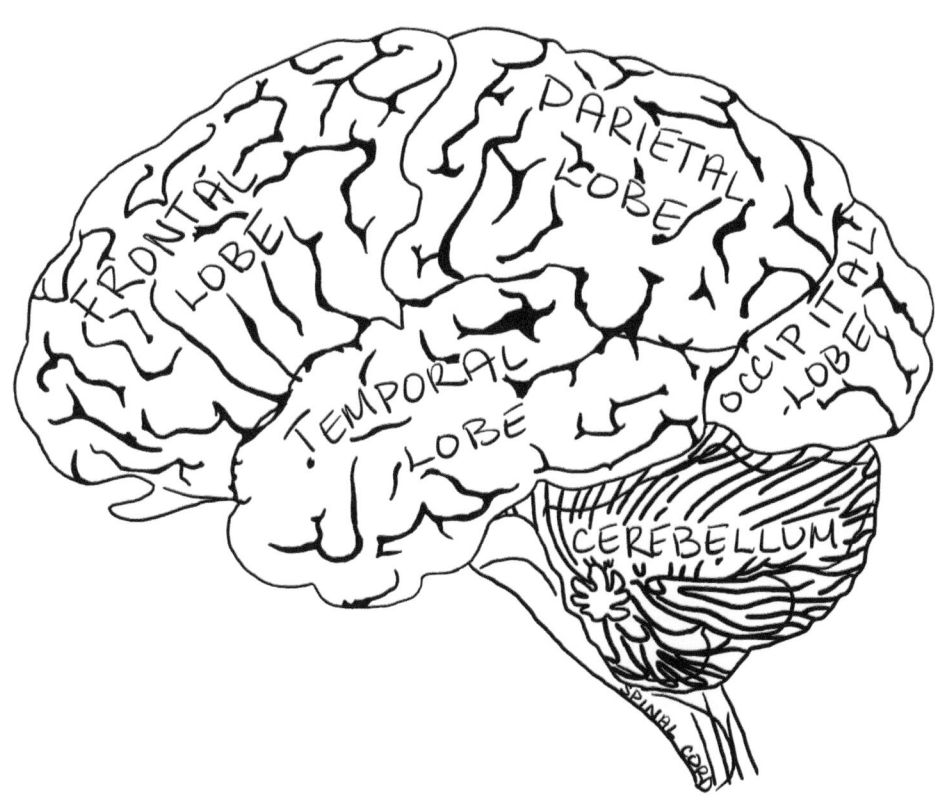

ALMOST DEAD

This is what happened: the Wednesday before Christmas 2021, while standing in my office in Downtown Portland, the room began to spin and I thought, here's another vertigo spell. I got dizzy and dropped to the floor and wanted to throw up. Judy and our daughter Audrey came to take me home. I went to bed where I struggled to get up.

Three days later on Christmas Day, I got out of bed and while opening presents, experienced another episode of heavy dizziness, thinking again, this is vertigo. I remember crying and going back to bed convinced I'd ruined Christmas.

The following Monday morning, I awoke with shooting pain emanating from the back left side of my neck, running down my left shoulder through my arm to my hand. A classic sign of a heart attack. I lay on the floor while Judy called 911. The EMTs brought me to the hospital. A CT-scan revealed a dissected left vertebral artery, one of the major arteries that carries blood to your brain.

A dissection is a split, in this case a tear in the inner-wall of the artery. A dissection usually occurs from some sort of head trauma—like what might occur in an automobile accident. I had no head trauma to report. The staff neurologist said the dissection might heal on its own, though sometimes clots form in the dissected area, so just to be careful he said and gave me blood-thinner pills and sent me home.

Over the previous ten years or so, it turns out, I had managed myself through a number of small strokes, which Judy and I thought were more and more episodes of vertigo. Vertigo is related to inner-ear issues, issues I'd been dealing with for some time, because of a hole in my right ear I'd had most of my life. I could hold my nose and close my mouth and blow air out my right ear. If I was hanging out near a friend smoking a cigarette, I could put the cigarette in my right ear, close my mouth, pinch my nose closed, and blow the air out until the end of the cigarette turned bright red.

HE'S DEAD

Throughout most of the past decade, every once in a while, I'd be standing or sitting and I'd black-out suddenly for a millisecond or so, then get nauseous and sometimes quite dizzy before dropping to the floor until I felt better. We thought I suffered vertigo. So though the attacks I'd had the week leading up to Christmas seemed more severe than prior ones, they were nothing I wasn't used to. But on the Tuesday after Christmas, Judy and I and our dear friend Joe were sitting on our couch when, as I described later to the doctors, I got walloped with a doozy to the brain. An overwhelming dizzy sensation knocked me down.

I looked at Judy, raised my hand, and said, "I'm done."

Then I blacked out.

No pulse. No breath. Eyes rolled to the back of my head.

Judy called 911. The EMTs came.

That's the day I died.

The EMTs and everyone in the medical profession would say otherwise, that I did not pass away.

I disagree.

HE'S NOT DEAD

Before the EMTs came, Judy later told me that she held on to my head and said, "Stay with me, Tom."

This was no fun for her. It was Hell.

I briefly woke up on the ER gurney to throw up. That's all I remember.

Because this was during COVID times, the nurses at the front desk wouldn't allow Judy or any non-patients in the hospital. Imagine that. You save your husband's life by getting the medics to him. You rush to the hospital and while he's undergoing brain surgery, the outcome of which is uncertain, the closest you can get to him is sitting in your car in the adjacent parking garage, crying and wondering.

THE JOURNEY

Two and a half years later, I think Judy may have some residual PTSD, though she's strong and would tell you otherwise.

I know I have PTSD.

I have for over two years.

Quite a journey.

POOP AND HURL

The hospital discharged me on New Year's Eve, 2021.

Judy picked me up, and we drove to the house we'd been renting while our home on Pine Street underwent renovations. Two of our kids returned home and caught the stomach flu, which I got almost immediately. I couldn't get to the bathroom without Judy's help. I didn't have much balance and couldn't take in any fluids. I sat slumped on the toilet with a red bucket in my hands, dry heaving into it and pooping soup, or at least something that looked like chicken broth.

The EMTs came to the house, took my vitals, and straighten me up, best they could.

The lead EMT said, "You sure you're not just having a bad day?"

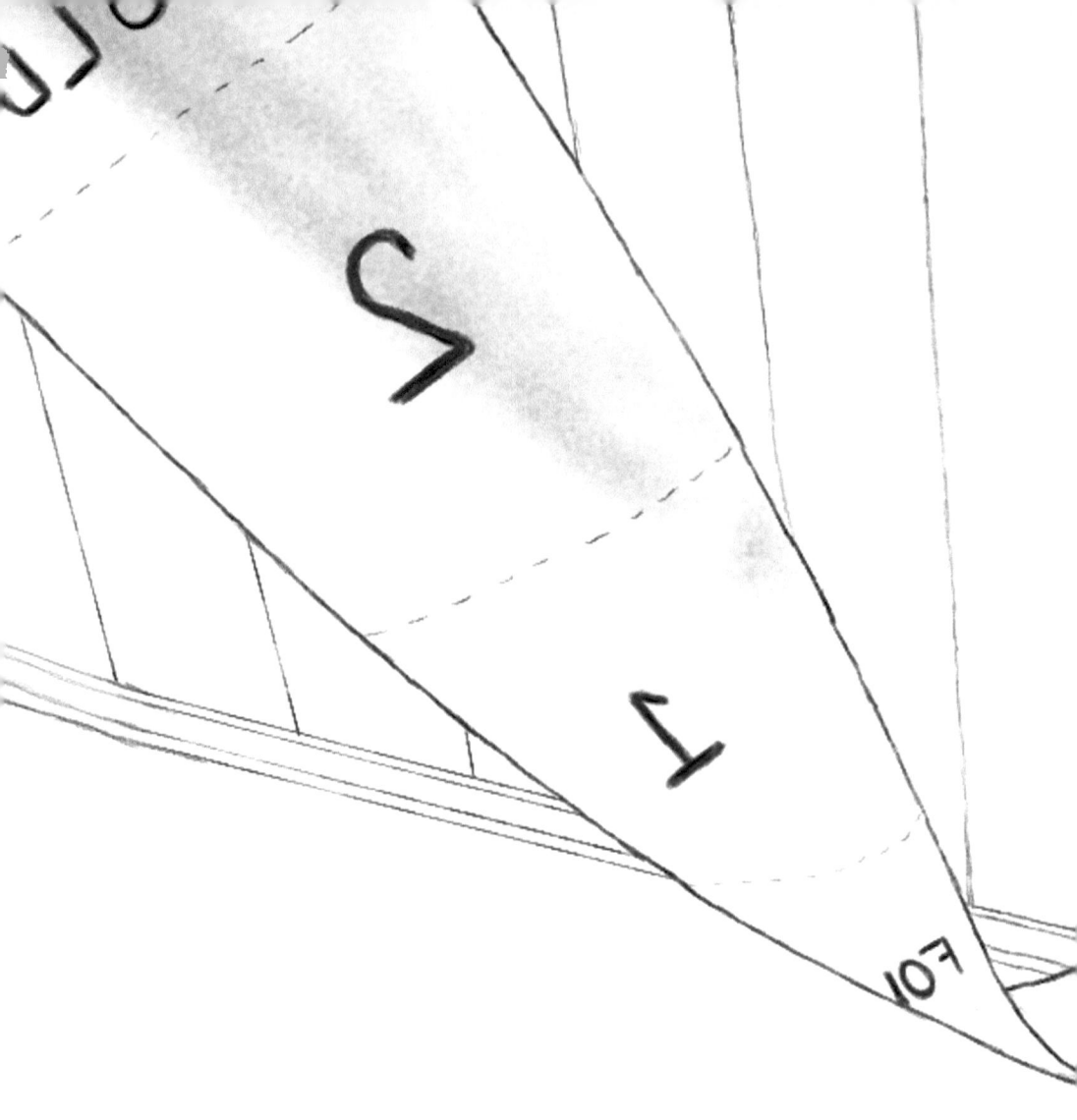

CAN YOU TAKE ME TO THE BATHROOM?

For a solid few months after that, Judy accompanied me to the bathroom. My equilibrium center had taken quite a hit so I more wobbled than walked. Judy worried I'd fall and knock myself dead by hitting my head on the sink or toilet.

I never did. I held onto the walls.

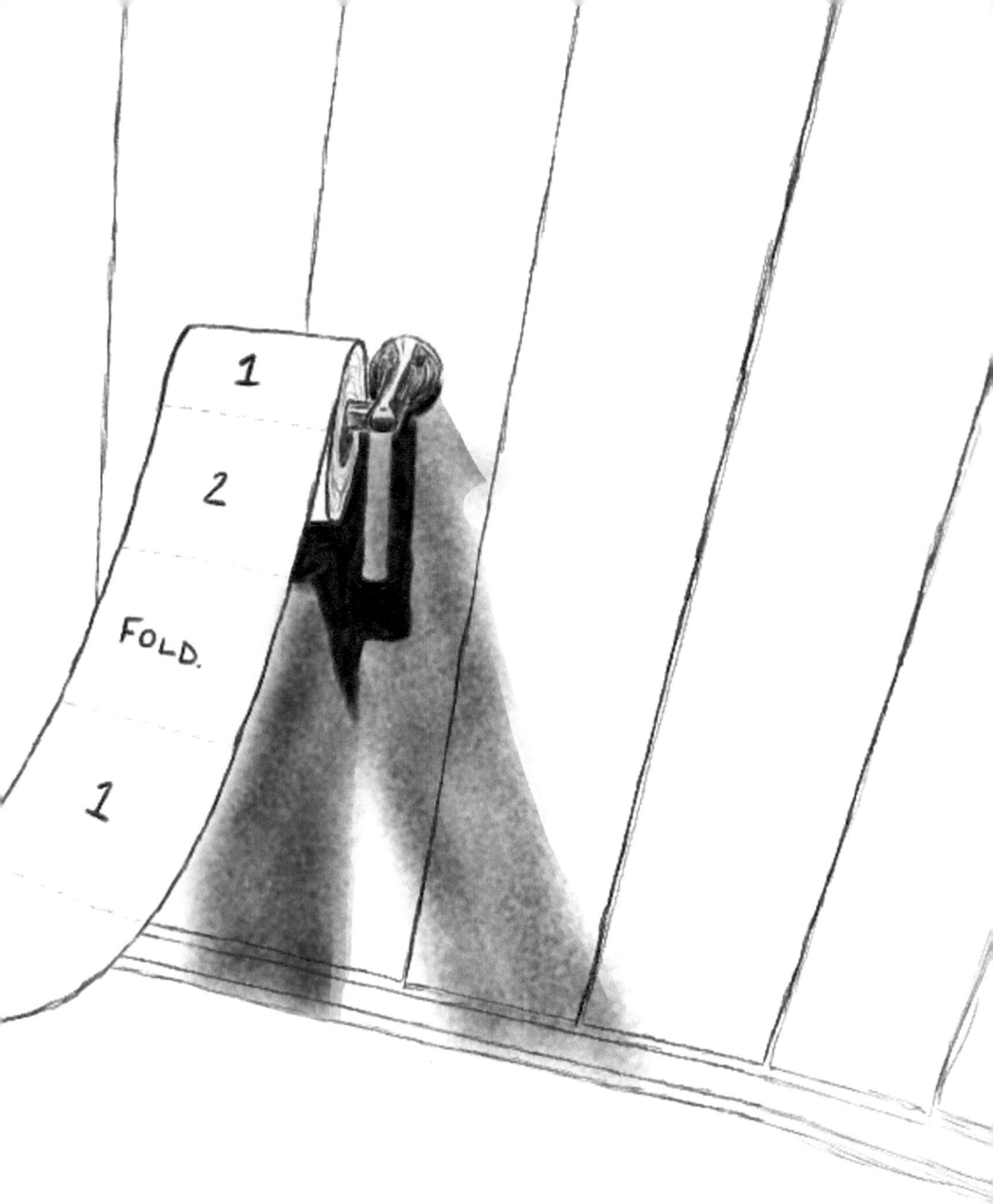

I'm pretty sure you don't ever want to accompany someone to the toilet.

Judy told me later, "I knew you were anal when you took only three squares of paper and folded them into one. Every time. And if you needed a second wipe, you'd do the same thing."

DON'T REMEMBER SHIT

The brain injury and stroke brought me to a place where I struggled to remember things. Judy accompanied me to my doctors' visits—and there were many those days: primary care physician, neurologist (Boston), neurologist (Portland), CT scan, MRI, urologist, neuro-optometrist, physical therapist, occupational therapist, speech therapist, otolaryngologist, neuropsychologist.

There are questions I had to ask the doctors, but I forgot them before arriving.

Judy didn't.

I didn't remember the results or the advice from the doctors later, either.

Judy wrote these notes down during the visits. I remember that.

CAN'T TIE MY SHOES

Unless you live with me, you wouldn't know I had this injury. It's invisible. Not like a broken leg. Judy lives with me. She sees it every day. Through the days and weeks, she still gets glimpses of my slurring speech, my struggle tying shoes. She sees me tightly grip the banister as I go down the stairs, occasionally hold on to the wall or countertop to be steady. She sees me taking the medications each morning and evening. She sees me pause during tasks to regain my energy and focus. Simple tasks like washing dishes, walking the dog, folding laundry, moving a chair from point A to B, talking on the phone.

Like I say, unless you lived with me—actually, unless you lived with me and you are Judy—you probably wouldn't see me as brain-injured, even though sometimes I walk into swinging doors. If you saw that, you'd begin to wonder.

TRIP BEGINS WITH A KISS

On the fifth day in the hospital, Judy and I finally got to hold hands and kiss. I didn't mind my time in the hospital. For the first time in over thirty years, I found myself away from work and the busy-ness. My nonstop life stopped. I enjoyed the quietude, but I missed Judy. I missed love. I missed her beautiful face and quick wit and her thoughtfulness and kindness. I missed hugs. The missing and the love far outweighed the solitude.

We first kissed in the early evening of August 15, 1998. On the corner of Carleton and Pine Streets in Portland's West End. I fell in love.

Judy is one of the most unique people I've ever met. She's smart, a very good writer, an IT brain; she's also fun and funny and likes to laugh. She can knit a blanket, sweat a copper pipe, hang a cabinet, and shake up a martini or Manhattan that you'll love.

We got married about a year after that first kiss.

It's been quite a trip.

FEAR AND WORRY

My equilibrium center took a beating from the blood clots, and we'd been warned about my risk of another episode. We didn't want that to happen. Anytime Judy left the house after that, she made sure someone came to walk or sit with me who could call the EMTs in case I relapsed. A great group of friends and family stayed with me through this scary time.

A lot of fear and worry.

Judy was patient with me while I tried to be a good patient. She studied what they told me to do in physical therapy sessions, and on off-days took me to Baxter Woods on Stevens Avenue and made sure I mimicked PT.

Walk: *head-up, head-down, look left, look right, reach up and touch the branch, reach down and touch the trunk, balance on this log.*

She observed me at home and saw that I got dizzy walking the dog.

Couldn't deal with lights from the TV.

Couldn't hold a conversation for more than a few minutes.

Couldn't keep myself from crying seemingly randomly.

And that scared me.

ATTEMPTED RUNNING

About six months after I got out of the hospital, I attempted some running.

Judy and I walked to Portland's Back Cove, which is circumnavigated by a 3 ½-mile long walking trail, lined on the non-water side with numbered linden trees, each number representing a Portland soldier killed in World War I. We mostly walked, though at about every fifth or sixth tree we ran to the next one.

After a few weeks, we began to run longer distances, up to a minute long. Judy played the role of the time-keeper with her watch. At some point, we ran partial quarter-miles, walking the other part. Judy is a fantastic athlete and an excellent coach, and while she can play most any sport as best as anyone, she doesn't like running for running's sake. She never took to our Back Cove excursions, but she very much took to my taking to it.

TRUE BELIEVER

After the brain injury, I found myself interested in a book of the stories of those who overcome adversity. At first, I got lightheaded and foggy after ten minutes of reading and had to put my reading down. But Glenn Mangurian's story inspired and moved me: in 2001 one of his discs ruptured, pressing against his spinal cord, rendering him paralyzed in the lower-half of his body.

He lives by his words:

"Those who have survived a traumatic life-altering event often convey a very curious sentiment: some people emerge from adversity—whether a career crisis or a devastating breakup or a frightening diagnosis—not just changed but stronger and more content. They seem to have found new peace and even an optimism that they didn't have before."

He goes on to say: "To survive, you need at least one true believer, someone who will have faith in your ability to recover, even when you lose it yourself."

Thank you, Judy.

THINGS COME APART

And you can put them back together. Though not always.

I knew nobody when I first moved to Portland in 1993, but I knew Rob and he knew everybody. A ton of energy. Gregarious. A quick wit and willing to do anything—like help me find my way professionally, geographically, socially.

Rob worked alongside me every day, neither of us knowing particularly at all what we were doing, or what we were going to do, but unafraid of anything.

We learned as we went. How to sweat pipes and fix electrical glitches. How to take things apart, replace the faulty piece, put things back together.

Rob was courageous and fearless, working with me long days and through weekends. We plunged toilets, replaced hot water heaters, installed new thermostats, flushed boilers, patched leaking roofs, cut grass, did grounds; installed new locks and dead bolts, new smoke and carbon-monoxide detectors. We snow-shoveled, snow-blowed, and salted and sanded.

Most businesses fail.

Either immediately or a bit later.

One fifth fail in the first year and half fail by year five.

After a certain amount of time a lot of folks just fold up shop. Call it. Cash it in.

THE START OF SOMETHING

The movie *Convoy*, which came out in 1978, is about a mile-long band of truckers scoring a grudge against an abusive sheriff. The main character, played by Kris Kristofferson and named Rubber Duck, and his buddies Pig Pen, Widow Woman, and Spider Mike are the notables in the convoy. Like all truckers before cell phones came into vogue, these folks rolled with "citizens band" radios, or CBs, in their trucks with which they communicated to each other, mostly about the presence of speed-traps.

The small band of people who helped me start what would later become a half-billion-dollar company, were known as the radio crew, because, like the truckers in *Convoy*, we needed to stay in touch all day. Back then cell phones hadn't been invented yet, and we were all working on different projects in buildings around town.

The Radio Crew—eighteen extraordinary humans who became my go-to team—helped get our business off the ground. The Crew, all of whom continue to be friends three decades later, took their work seriously but didn't take themselves too seriously. They did everything they could each day to make sure things didn't go wrong. But of course, things did. Buildings have lots of moving parts and people living in them. We worked all hours, nights and weekends.

"Please, come quick."

This is what the Crew did.

We were a comedy troupe of brash, independent people who didn't want to follow the corporate path, or go to college, or get a "real job," but wanted demanding and sometimes very physical work with a small band of others. Maybe we were all outsiders.

INTRODUCING THE RADIO CREW

It was an FCC regulation that you couldn't use your real name, so we referred to ourselves with "handles."

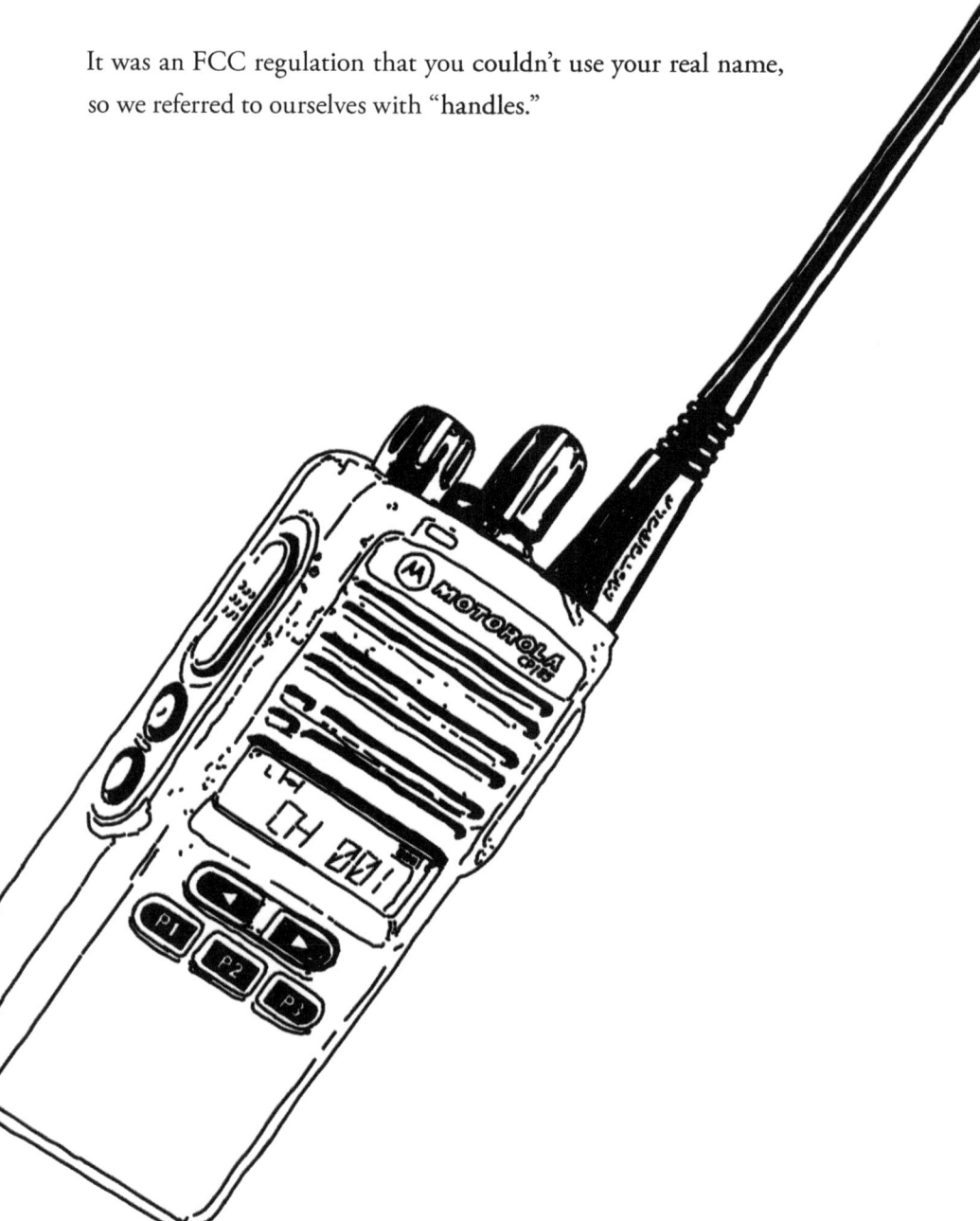

Judy:	maiden name fisher	fishcakes
Tom:	take on "shamu" the whale	wabu
Leyli:	the instrument, ukulele	euka
Lucy:	grew up in blue hill	blue
Maureen:	color of her hair	cherry
Mark:	the youngest in his family	baby
Joe:	our carpenter	woody
Darien:	a fierce and intriguing musician	winking tiger
Mike:	many superpowers	green lantern
Daryl:	operated the plow truck	snowman
Sarah:	in multiple car accidents	crash
Shawn:	the power of the peak	shawnee peak
Lynn:	sky's the limit	sky
Jackie:	my little sister	wenchy
Russell:	rhymes with	muscle
Paul:	"flower boy," did grounds	flobo
Dad:	owned a boat	captain jack
Bob:	an Andy Kaufman character	rico suave

YOU OPEN A BAKERY

I started my business in 1993 out of the back of my pick-up truck, not knowing a thing. Maybe that's why we took on so many seemingly impossible reclamation projects. I had no idea what I was doing. Why should that stop me? Why should that stop any of us?

Most folks starting a business are taking on a lot of risk. They're about to do a bunch of things they've never done before, like manage employees, hire people, fire people, lose sleep over a lack of cash, worry about an unhappy customer or client. You open a bakery, and you think you're going to bake cakes most of the day, but you find yourself marketing, doing books, paying bills, and wondering why your worker didn't show up this morning.

There's so much liability: financial risk, reputational risk, home life.

A small business is usually started by just one person with an idea and some guts, and this one person (times all the small businesses that exist) employs almost half the American workforce. There's an enormous amount of responsibility that goes with that. And there are always a lot of problems and troubles to solve.

SINK HOLE

The second building I bought in Portland was 122-124 Brackett Street. Many of the tenants from the first building we bought on 204 Spring Street parked in the 122 lot. One guy drove a semi. This is a big truck. Not one you would park in a residential neighborhood. This truck created a very large hole in the middle of the parking lot. His front left tire got stuck in it.

He called it a "sink hole."

THREE I.V. BAGS, PLEASE

Like a lot of buildings, 285 Bracket Street, a twelve-unit building on the edge of Portland's West End, was originally a six-unit. My dad and I bought the building on June 1, 1994, and by the end of the month we were renovating. At some point in the 1970s, the landlord had decided to split each big unit into two smaller units which meant, among other issues, new bathrooms needed to be installed, one in each unit. They did this the cheapest way possible: put in flimsy, thin metal booth-like shower stalls, not attached to the wall but close to a corner to meet the pipes traveling up the back of it. You could shake these stalls. They were that rickety. We called them camp showers. Among the several fixes we planned on, we were determined to create nice bathrooms with real showers.

Apartment Number 9 sits on the left side, second floor. I ripped out the metal camper shower in there and built walls with 2x4s and sheet rock, then installed a new fiberglass shower stall with the plumbing hidden in the new walls but for where it stubbed out into the shower. This was a small, windowless space in the middle of the building where no air circulated and the heat rose steadily. I was sweating quite a lot during the work and tiring. I drank several cups of iced coffee the last day to keep myself going while my shirt soaked through, and my pants stuck to me.

At some point in the early evening, we called it a day and went to play ultimate frisbee at Payson Park, just off the peninsula abutting the Back Cove. We played in the heat and humidity for a few hours until the sun went down, then drove to one of Portland's long-time popular pubs, Gritty's, where we enjoyed each other's company over beers and tequila shots. The next day I could not get out of bed.

Apparently, I'd done everything possible the previous day to bring on heat exhaustion:

> I'd overdressed
> I got dehydrated
> I played a sport strenuously in the heat and humidity
> I drank alcohol.

I lay in bed in my closet in the Spring Street apartment, dizzy.

I couldn't take in fluids. I couldn't eat anything. My father came and took me to the hospital where they administered three bags of IV. They were very kind in explaining what I'd done to myself.

I'd like to say that never happened again.

FLEA BOMBS AWAY!

When we bought 240-242 Brackett Street in July of 1994, it had mint green vinyl siding. Still does. Once we finished the renovations, my buddy Patrick and I moved into the second floor two-bedroom apartment. Fleas were flying all around, so we set off a couple of "flea bombs" to get rid of the stragglers.

"Flea bombs away!" we yelled and ran out the door.

THIS IS RISK

90 Pine Street is a four-unit, square, yellow, flat-rooved building on the corner of Pine and Lewis Streets in Portland's West End. My dad and Judy and I bought it in 2009 after it was foreclosed upon by the bank. My guess is given how unsafe it was (not at all up to code), the bank evicted the tenants to avoid liability. Or perhaps the tenants left on their own because the heat had been turned off, the electrical service was intermittent, and the basement flooded.

For over a year it sat vacant, clad in anemic, light-blue vinyl siding. Inside, the apartments were trashed, and by that I mean ripped apart: holes in walls, doors off hinges or missing, copper pipes gone (probably due to theft), cabinets, fixtures, and toilets all gone too, and a sewer stink emanating from each open waste pipe.

Our good friend Mark, or "Baby" as was his radio handle, ran the renovation. He painted the outside bright yellow, the vibrancy of which to this day catches your eye. Our friend Nate from Westbrook installed multiple kitchens. It was a lot of work and a lot of money. This is risk—wondering if anyone would move into a small, shuttered, abandoned apartment house. And if no one would, well, we still owed the bank every month.

Could we stop the water from coming into the basement? Could we get rid of the sewage smell, the mold, and the must? Could we make the place safe, clean, and attractive?

Uncertain as we were, this was risk we were willing to take and, as best we could tell, others were not. Probably with good reason. The smell alone would have driven most people away.

THAT'S MY WIFE

"That bowling ball, that's my wife!"
J. Geils Band, "No Anchovies, Please"

Right around the time our daughter Audrey was born, my partner Brian and I purchased 63-77 Danforth, between Portland's West End and the Old Port, a stretch known for its shopping, bars and restaurants. The property consisted of six buildings—forty apartments—all in rough shape. Very rough shape. The worst we'd ever purchased.

In late November of 2003, Judy placed Audrey alongside her older sister Rose in daycare. Our neighbor, Stuart, had recently graduated from high school and was eager to work, so Judy, age thirty-seven at the time, and Stuart, age nineteen, did all the renovations on the Danforth apartments—an exceptional amount of work to complete for just one apartment. They did them all.

Bill at TD Bank had loaned us the money to buy the Danforth apartments, and I wanted to show him the progress we were making. He and I walked up one day from the Old Port where Bill's office was and stood on the sidewalk opposite the building. Judy happened to be carrying a 4x8, ¾-inch thick piece of plywood—a heavy piece of plywood awkward to move—up the steep entrance stairway. Most times you'll see two construction guys carrying one piece like this, a guy at each end. I looked at Bill, amazed at her feat, and said, "Oh my God, that's my wife!"

POOP FLUSH, WIPE FLUSH

After the new low-flush toilet came out, we made it our company logo in the '90s, emblazoned in big brown letters on the backs of our bright yellow company shirts: poop flush, wipe flush.

One low flush flushed 1.6 gallons down the waste pipe, as compared to the then current standard toilet which flushed around four times that amount.

Apparently 1.6 gallons got your business down and out the toilet.

We installed new ones everywhere. But it turned out one flush lacked sufficiency, leaving a portion of your business sitting in the bowl. It took two flushes.

Tenants called us.

> Yes, we know, you have to poop flush, wipe flush.
> Yes, well, no, it's not absurd.

Actually, it was absurd.

So we made it our company motto.

LEYLI IS DWAYNE SCHNEIDER

Leyli, one of the first of the original radio crew, worked with me for over twenty-five years as our only maintenance tech and eventually became head of our 10-person maintenance department when the company grew. Most trades folks are men. Plumbers, boiler repairmen, electricians, roofers. But not Leyli. She put her brilliance to work every day—more so than most men she worked with. She diagnosed things carefully, thoughtfully and accurately and then she fixed them. By her force of personality and willingness to get her hands dirty, sexism faded away around her or died a quick death. She and the multiple tradesmen, and yes, they were all men, became fast friends.

In the mid-1970s, a sitcom about a divorced mom and her two teenage daughters living in an apartment complex aired weekly. The maintenance man, Dwayne Schneider, fancied himself suave, though he usually bumbled and mis-stepped. Still, he was an endearing character. Portland had a popular local newspaper then known as the *Casco Bay Weekly*, and in early 1996 the paper did a piece about Leyli: a woman doing what was "historically a man's job."

The title of the article: "Schneiderilla."

LEYLI IS INSISTENT

While it took some time, maybe a couple of years, people grew accustomed to flushing the toilet twice.

The water bills that we paid to the Portland water district dropped dramatically, close to half. As a landlord, this was exciting stuff. Saving water. Saving money.

Everybody wins.

Most of us on the radio crew, struggled with Leyli's insistence that if tenants only peed, they should not flush. Everyone knew, and most everyone knows, that a bowl of unflushed pee stinks exponentially over time. Still Leyli stood firm in her insistence.

NERVOUS DOWNTOWN

We bought the Metropolitan in 2000, an eighty-one-unit apartment building with four commercial storefronts at 439 Congress Street in Portland's Monument Square. The building was in rough shape and housed yet a rougher crowd, and they could be mean. Not just to me, but to each other.

The heat pipes and radiators clanged at all hours, the windows leaked cold air, and the bathrooms and kitchens looked to be 1950s, vintage: smoked-stained walls, plywood cabinets and countertops. Each floor consisted of seventeen apartments, including the top floor; though oddly, no one seemed to have lived on that floor for years. So that's where we started.

The whole radio crew came to the Metro that first day, even Sky, our normally desk-bound accountant. There were probably twenty of us. This was the first downtown building we'd ever bought, and we were—all of us—excited and nervous: excited, because it was a new adventure for us and we were hopeful we could make the apartments nice; nervous, because we were going to spend a lot of time, energy and money on renovating apartments we weren't sure anyone would rent, there being no parking.

We put a large dumpster beside the Unitarian church next door and chucked everything out the windows into it. By the end of the first day, the nervousness in all of us seemed to have subsided, one of the benefits, no doubt, of chucking heavy items out of fifth-story windows. The apartments had great bones: tall ceilings, big windows, hardwood floors. Now we were confident we'd make them beautiful.

SLEEP STANDING UP

In 2005, we bought 485 Cumberland Avenue, known as the Copeley. It was a twenty-six-unit building that must still have the smallest apartments in the city at 150 square feet, with bathrooms occupying close to half that space. The property was full of cockroaches and smelled like throw-up and decaying food. The hallways felt dark and threatening. And the units that hadn't been lived in for years, and maybe couldn't have been, given how ruined they were, made the property feel like a flop house.

We threw out nearly everything: malfunctioning toilets and smelly carpets and discarded mattresses. We sheet-rocked and painted the walls, installed kitchens and baths, put in new lighting. We installed a new heating system and new fire alarm system and made the electrical work safe. We replaced all the windows, sanded the wood floors, and polyurethaned them. In many of the kitchens, due to their small size, we installed in-counter hot plates; no room for a full stove. Same with the refrigerators: we slid miniature ones under the counter; microwaves tucked into the upper-kitchen cabinet. Between the bathroom and the kitchen there remained very little room for what you'd normally appoint an apartment with: a table, a chair, a desk, a bureau, and a bed. Something had to be left out. Sleep on a couch maybe?

Our advertisement in the local paper read: "If you can sleep standing up, we've got the apartment for you."

SHE'S SERIOUS THIS TIME

I struggled collecting rent from truant tenants.

Too sympathetic.

Still, the bank wanted their money.

My mortgage came due the first of every month, and if the bank didn't get their payment, they penalized me, heftily. If they wanted to, they could even foreclose and take the building.

I hired Lynn, who went by the radio handle "Sky." She's brilliant and to the point, to this day. She grew up in Riverside, in the low-income housing projects, got married young and had a daughter. When she came to work for me, she was a single mom and adamant I pay insurance to cover her and her young child, which I did.

I overheard her once through the office wall: "Either you pay your rent, or I lose my job and I'm not going to lose my job."

She meant it.

TWO MONTHS LATE

Lynn is also one of the funniest people I know: quick, witty, hilarious.

L: So, Tom, who is this guy, Alex?

T: My friend.

L: How do you know him?

T: Frisbee. He's the captain of my frisbee team.

L: So, people who play frisbee don't have to pay rent?

T: No, they do.

L: He's thirty-five days late. Which means he owes last month and this month.

T: Ok, thank you. I'll talk to him.

L: Don't thank me. He's your friend.

THIS IS WHAT YOU TELL HIM

T: Alex, you need to pay me rent, dude. Like now.

A: So official. I'll be right down.

T: Thanks.

A: Here it is.

T: This just covers last month. What about this month's rent?

D: Dude, get off my back. I'm only five days late.

Alex and I continue to be great friends.

LEYLI BELIEVES IN GHOSTS

Leyli and I agreed on a lot more things than we disagreed, but when we disagreed, it could be time-consuming. At some point in the mid 1990s, a tenant on the second floor of 122-124 Brackett Street called me to tell me that the building shook a lot—that it had shaken that morning. Leyli and I investigated.

We wondered, could it be wind? Maybe the property got caught in some sort of cross current, it being on a corner. But there'd been no wind that day and no bad weather. No big trucks regularly drove past. No bus route. The planes from the airport flew along the Fore River, many blocks away, and the trains were in another part of the city.

> It's ghosts then, Leyli said. You need to call her and tell her it's ghosts. That's common in these old buildings.
>
> I'm not going to call her and tell her the building is haunted. It's not ghosts.
>
> It is. That's what it is.
>
> I'm not telling her that.

A couple weeks later the first floor apartment came vacant, so I went to paint it and polyurethane the wood floors. I kept the windows and door open. Two tenants came down from the third floor to say hello and see my progress. They were a very large young man and very large young woman holding hands and quite amorous towards each other. They left.

Oh, I thought, Leyli's ghosts.

ON THE ROOF AT NIGHT IN AN ICE STORM

Leyli got a call one night in mid-February from a tenant living on the top floor of 285 Brackett Street asking her to please come over to see the water leaking through her ceiling. Judy and I went to help and found Leyli already on the roof with a shovel and an axe. Access to the roof required placing an extension ladder on the rear outside fire escape, which she'd done at night alone during an ice storm.

About eight inches of standing water was pooled on the roof, so Judy grabbed the shovel and started scooping water and throwing it off the edge to the ground below. No guard rail. Thirty-five-foot drop. Again, this was at night, during a storm.

Flat roofs pitch inward to the center of the building to a drain that takes rainwater and ice melt down through the building to the basement where it connects from the main exit waste line to the sewer line in the street. The drain on this roof had iced over.

Leyli and I hacked at the ice and snow on the grate atop the drainpipe, while the wind whipped in our faces. We had headlamps on and moved fast, while Judy did an amazing job throwing off water. When Leyli and I broke through, ice and water rushed down.

The leak stopped.

NAIL STRAIGHT THROUGH HER FOOT

My dad and I had bought 240-242 Brackett Street in the early 1990s after a SWAT team's drug-bust there. Three of the four apartments were empty and full of fleas and feral cats. Lots of broken windows. Empty vodka bottles strewn about. In the fourth apartment, a one-bedroom on the first floor, lived four guys and three dogs, the latter of which were allowed to romp around freely and defecate prolifically in the backyard, a backyard once home to grass and flowers, now to poop, pee and trodden dirt, hard and stinky.

The guys couldn't understand why I wanted them to move out.

I asked nicely.

They were cool and moved. Probably happy to.

Shawnee Peak, Green Lantern, Leyli and I did the work: floor-sanding, wall repair, painting, pest eradication. We installed new windows, new locks to make it safe, bringing back the yard with grass and flowers, and a picnic table. The basement, with its one dim bulb and dirt floor, teemed with stacks of stuff various tenants left behind over the years.

We made several trips to the dump in two pick-up trucks to clear it out. At some point, Leyli stepped on a nail. Went through her boot and most of her foot. In a ton of pain and laid up for a few weeks, she took it stoically and complained not once.

My dad and I bought her an electric drill.

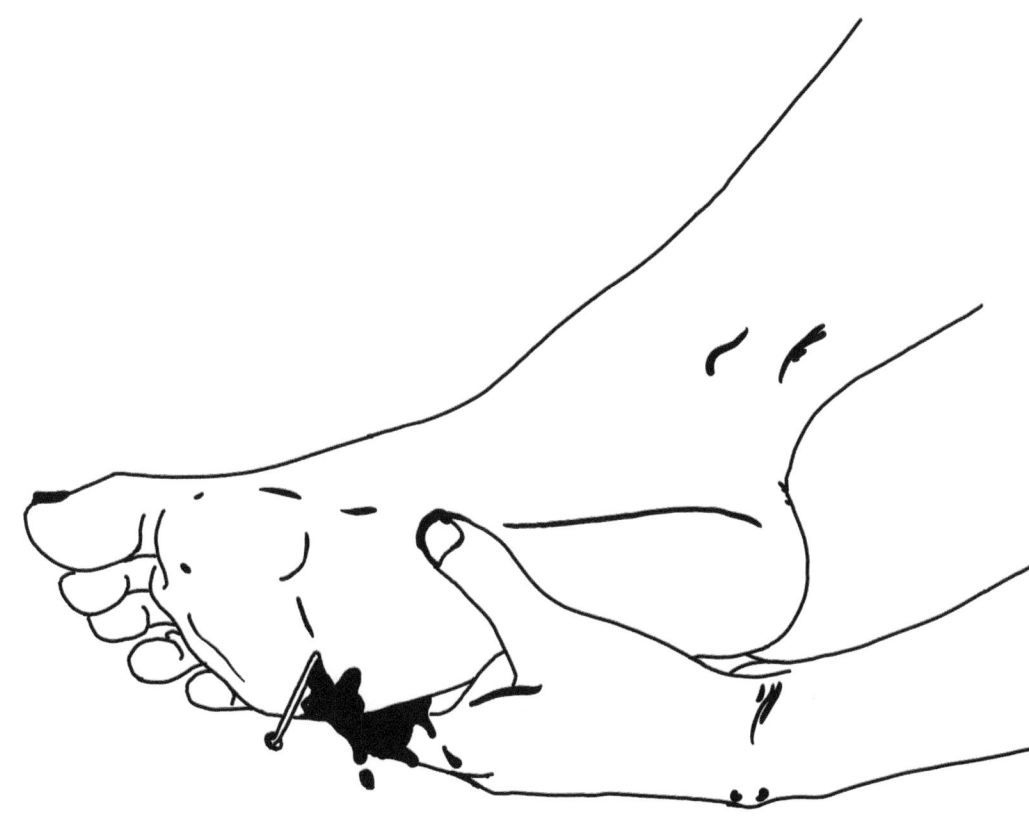

DIRTY EYES

Leyli came to spend a lot of time in basements. That's where everything comes into the building and where everything leaves the building.

Electricity, gas, oil, water come in; exhaust from burnt fuel and wastewater go out.

Our buildings were heated by large boilers anywhere from three-feet tall, two-feet wide to six-feet tall and six-feet wide. They're big. And they're called boilers because that's exactly what they do. The boiler has a waterline connected to it that fills it with water. An oil burner attached to the front bottom of the boiler takes in oil from an oil-line connected to the oil tank, then burns the oil to create a flame, which is often a furious and continuous jet of flame that shoots into the boiler to heat the water.

In a steam system, the water is boiled. In a forced hot water system, the water is heated to about 120 degrees. The steam or the hot water travels to the radiators or baseboard heaters in the apartments that then get warm from the radiant heat. The oil burner has an eye, a piece of glass covering a sensor that shuts off the burner if it sees no flame. The boiler then shuts down to prevent oil from going into the boiler, unburned, where it could leak out of the bottom of the boiler on to the basement floor. If a full oil tank leaked, when such a leak occurred the basement was flooded with oil.

More often than not, in fact almost always, the problem with the boiler was that the eye didn't see the flame because it was covered with black soot. A dirty eye shut things down. Tenants called us about a loss of heat. Their apartment became cold. No heat emanated from their radiators. Oil, unlike natural gas, creates a black smoke. Soot even. Any downdraft (like you might experience on a cold windy day) from the roof down the chimney to the boiler's flue, can send black soot from the exhaust backwards and cover the eye. Leyli knew why the boiler shut down and you had no heat. She became a pro at cleaning dirty eyes.

Heat's back on.

YES, LEYLI IS A WOMAN

So, you said Larry will meet me in the basement?

No, I said Leyli. She's a woman.

Does she know what she's doing?

Go see for yourself.

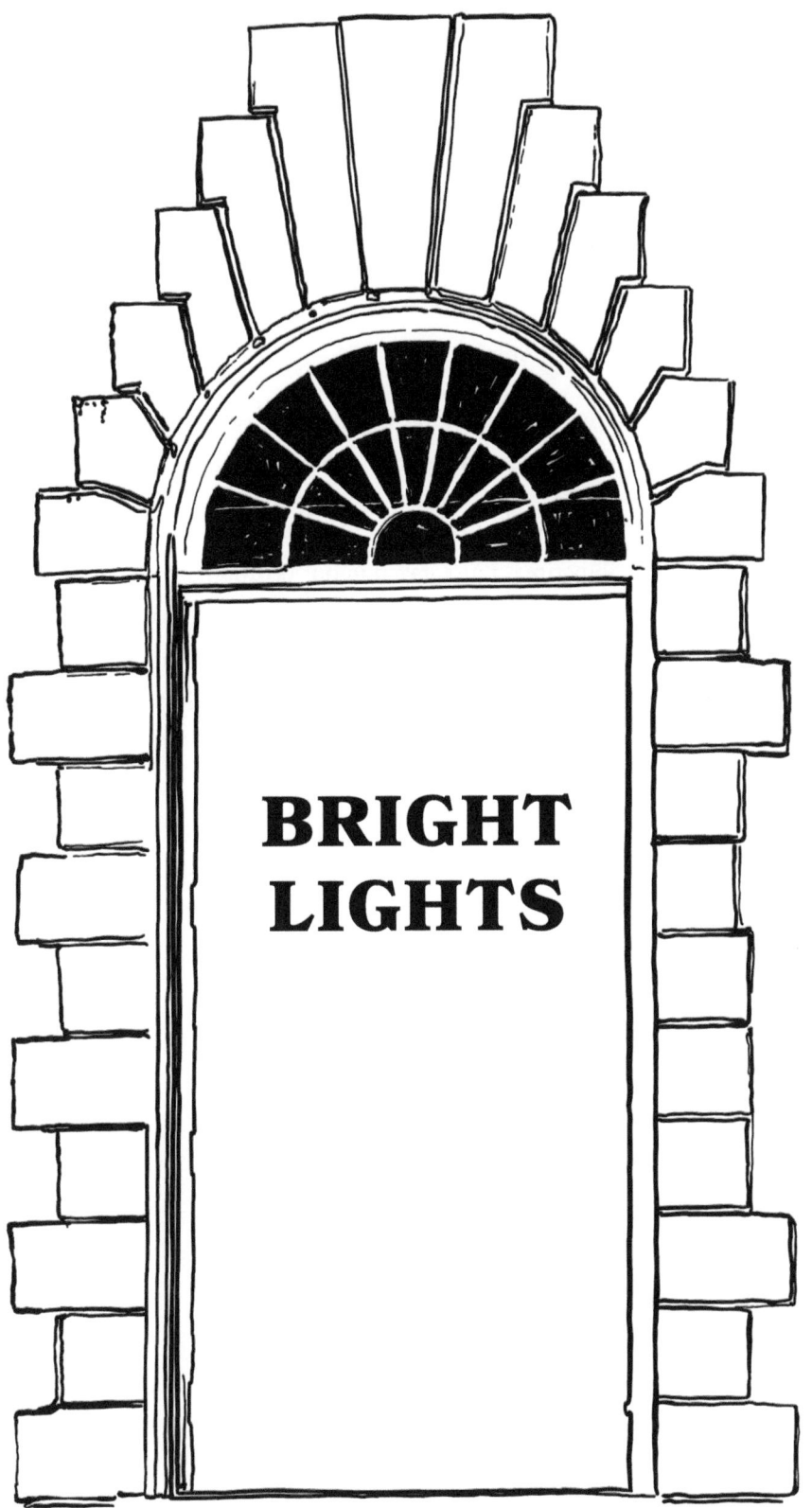

BRAIN INSULT

My surgeon says what I have is a "brain insult."

Call it what you want, it's an injury.

For a solid number of months, I couldn't stop myself from crying. I wasn't crying for any specific reason. I tried to do it out of sight so I wouldn't burden anyone.

I don't mind crying, and I don't mind seeing someone cry, but this was something like five times a day. Sometimes I just stayed in our bedroom by myself to cry. Got it out, and came out to watch a game. But I had trouble doing that too—I couldn't watch much TV because: 1, the lights were too bright, and 2, I found myself getting emotional about everything; even car chases made me worry and cry.

I developed this thing called supermarket syndrome too.

If I walked into the grocery store with Judy, I left pretty much immediately: too much light, color, choices and activity. This is a real thing, that's what it's called, supermarket syndrome. I waited in the car.

A lot of very good doctors helped me:

    The surgeon, Dr. S.

    Two neurologists
    (one in Boston, one in Portland)

    Two neuropsychologists
    (one for my anxiety, the other evaluating my progress)

    A psychologist

    My primary care physician

    Our brilliant osteopath

That's eight. All communicating and wisely advising me based on their field of expertise. All good people. I felt lucky.

SUPERMARKET SYNDROME

"Do you dread going to the grocery store because it makes you feel bad? The maze of tall shelves, the bright lights, patterns on the floor, the overwhelming selection of items, bending down or turning your head to scan for the items you need can take a lot of energy to navigate. If you can relate, you are not alone and there is nothing 'wrong' with you."

Vestibular.org

LOSING TRACK

Neuropsychological evaluation
4/19/2022

Current cognitive symptoms: Short term memory loss, losing track of topics when talking; word retrieval difficulties, difficulty making decisions, less automatic thinking.

Current physical symptoms: Fatigue; occasional lightheadedness/dizziness, reduced mental and physical endurance; occasional headaches; left hand pinky and fourth finger weakness.

Current emotional symptoms: Mood fluctuation; anxiety, worry, social anxiety, feelings of overwhelm at times.

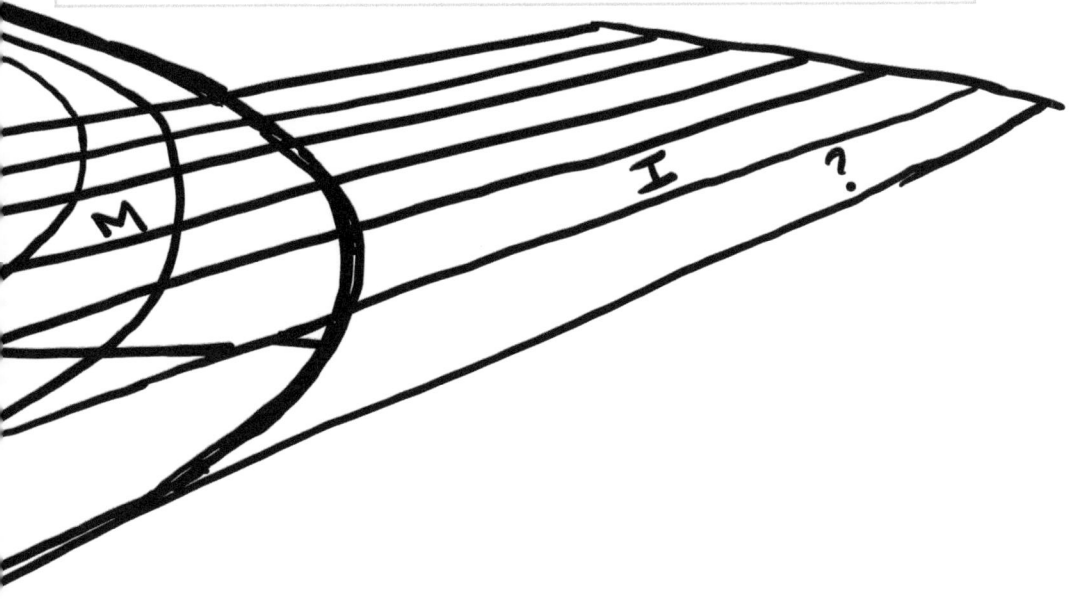

PROFOUND VERTIGO

Neuropsychological evaluation
4/19/2022

Mr. Watson returned to the emergency department on 12/28/21 with profound vertigo, nausea, vomiting, dysarthria, left facial droop, ataxia, and left gaze preference. Cerebral angiogram demonstrated as posterior cerebral artery distribution stroke.

Dysarthria = slurred speech.

Ataxia = impaired balance or coordination.

ALCOHOL

May 2, 2022
Dr. P.

"Tom has enjoyed generally good health over the years. He probably has long-term hypertension which he has been resistant to treat until recently. He also admits to alcohol overuse prior to his stroke and has cut way down on intake. There is no definitive family history of stroke. He describes himself as a fairly high-energy and intense person. Operates his own business."

ENERGY

May 2, 2022
Dr. P.

"He tells me that his energy level is quite good; since he has cut way down on alcohol use his sleep has improved. He tells me he has always had issues with anxiety and depression although these did seem quite a bit more problematic after his stroke."

OCCLUSION

> CT Scan
>
> May 5, 2022
>
> Mass General/Brigham and Women's Hospital
>
>
> Left vertebral artery: again, noted there is occlusion* of the left vertebral artery...likely representing low flow.
>
> *occlusion = partially or fully-closed

The doctors and just about anyone in medicine will tell you: should blood flow to your brain be reduced due to some event, your blood will figure out a way to regain that flow. You are not told how or how long that might take.

CRYING

Dr. F., Neurologist
Mass General/Brigham
Encounter date: 3/3/2022

He feels that he is quite anxious.

His mood is usually "all over the map," but now he is crying more.

LAUGHING

Neuropsychological evaluation
Mental status and behavioral observations
April 19, 2022

He worked diligently without complaint.

He fatigued but persisted to task.

He began laughing on an executive function task in which he had trouble processing efficiently.

THE FUTURE

Neuropsychological evaluation
April 19, 2022

Mr. Watson experiences dizziness and lightheadedness episodically and does not associate them with any activity. He reported increased emotionality since his stroke. He becomes activated easily and his blood pressure increases in context of happy or exciting news as well as more stressful interactions.

He reported feeling down at times and has experienced mood fluctuations.

He worries about his health and the future.

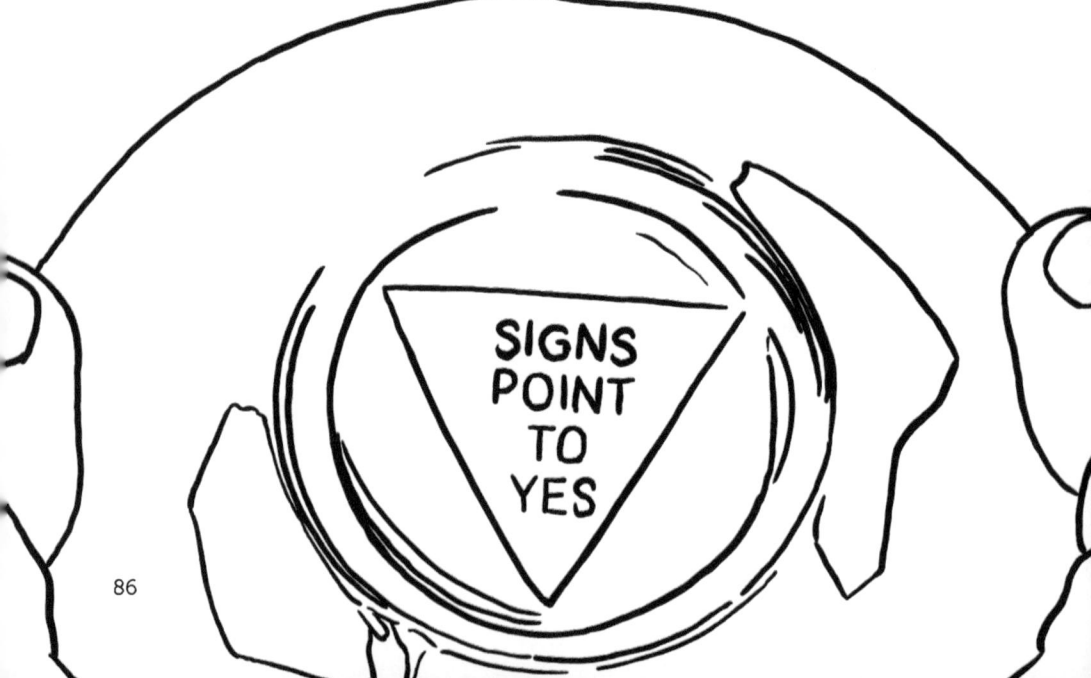

DEAR ROSE AND AUDREY

Sunday 4.17.2022
Portland, Maine

Forgive me if I'm telling you too much, but I've had to get this stuff, this internalized dialogue (so, monologue?) out in the open. It's just a bit weird and definitely difficult to live in semi-fog. I'll explain the fog here: because the blood clot took out my equilibrium center—or part of it—in my brain, I'm dizzy a lot and so I spend a lot of time—all day—trying to not be dizzy. I try to walk straight, turn around without falling down, pick something up from the ground without feeling nauseous, keep my head straight up, listen, talk, think, reason, relate. And it's hard work. Trying to maintain equilibrium consciously when normally it's done automatically, unthinking.

Here's where the fogginess kicks in: I'm trying to listen, while also trying to pay attention, while suppressing the dizziness.

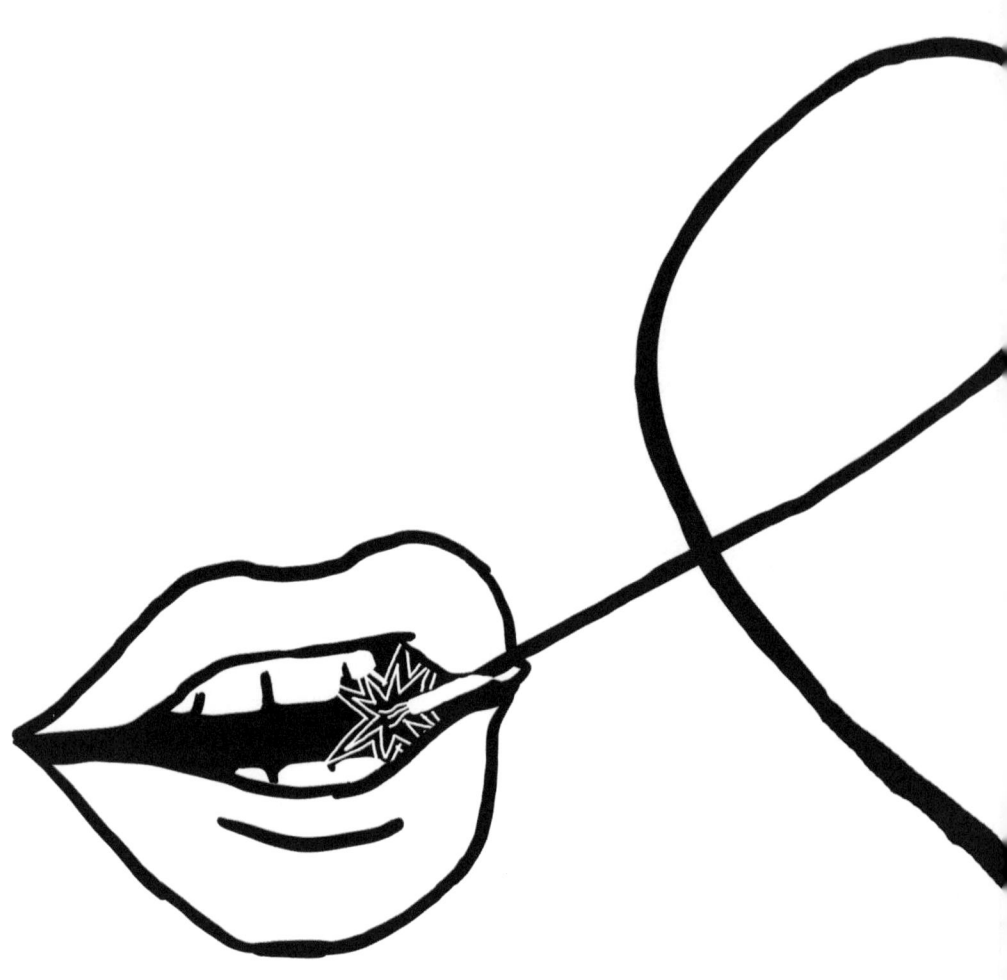

LEYLI IS SHOCKED!

In January of 1994, we bought our third property in Portland, a twenty-six-unit brick building at 288 State Street just across from Deering Oaks Park. The resident manager who'd been living there saw our enthusiasm to start cleaning up the dilapidated apartments and told us very seriously, "There is no way you can buff these turds."

These were big apartments that needed a lot of work to become beautiful. We rented floor sanders from a local machine rental store called Handyman Rental, and the sanding created a thick dust that we breathed in. We didn't know dust masks were a thing and that you could buy them at the same place you rented the sander, so we just took off our T-shirts and wore them as bandanas around our noses and mouths.

Rob and I were sanding the floors in a corner unit one day, and Leyli was doing some maintenance next to us when a dangling live wire caught her directly in the mouth. She went down to the ground.

Imagine an electric shock through your teeth, your tongue, and the roof of your mouth. She sat there and let the shock work its way out.

DOGGIE DNA

People won't tell you this, but if you have a dog in the city, you know when he or she is going to poop or needs to poop. You're picking up their poop one or two times a day every day. Knowing their habits may not be one you boast about or talk about. Still, city dog owners know the signs, most notably the pursed sphincter. For my dog Stark—I bring three bags when we go for a walk as he has occasionally performed the trifecta. If not three, he's good for two. The deuce caboose.

In the 1990s and early 2000s on the peninsula, as best I can recall, people didn't pick up after their dogs. During the winter at night or during inclement weather, folks commonly stood in the entry doorway and let their dog out to do its business.

When the snow melted in late March or early April, all the dog poop hidden by the snow appeared. Poop on poop on poop. Tons of it. Melting.

Leyli made the decision in the early 2000s that, as landlords, we would no longer allow dogs in our apartments based on what happened when the snow melted. The problem, we discovered within a year of the new rule, is that we lost nearly half of our potential market. To be a bit hyperbolic, almost everyone had a dog, and most dog owners were responsible people, the kind you wanted living in your building. We changed policy. Not quite an about-face. Leyli would now interview the dog.

As a potential tenant interested in renting one of our apartments, if you had a dog, we asked that you bring the dog to the office so Leyli could meet him or her. As head maintenance tech, Leyli often entered apartments when the tenant wasn't there but the dog was, and she found herself too often not well-received. The dogs were territorial and wouldn't let her in.

Along with the interview, she swabbed the dogs' mouths and sent the saliva sample to the lab for recording—the concern being that no tenant would admit to their dog pooping on our property. Now we could take a sample of the poop and send it to the lab to find a match. The problem? None of us, including Leyli, wanted to take a poop sample. The interview worked out great. The DNA sampling, not so much.

DOG POOP

Sec. 5-71 Duty to Dispose.

It shall be a violation of this division for any person who owns, possesses or controls a dog to fail to remove and dispose of any feces left by his/her dog on any sidewalk, street, or publicly owned property.

Sec. 5-73 Enforcement.

The provisions of this division may be enforced by any designated representative of the director of parks and recreation or, the chief of police, or by the canine control officer.

Sec. 5-74 Penalties for Violation.

Violation of this division shall be punished by a minimum penalty of two hundred and fifty dollars ($250.00) for each violation. The minimum penalty for a third offense under this section shall be five hundred dollars ($500.00). Where financial hardship is demonstrated, a violator of this division may perform community service in lieu of the financial penalty, if such a program is available through the city. Such community service shall consist of removing canine waste within the city at a rate of 25 hours per offense and 50 hours for the third (or more) offense.

Sec. 5-75 Exemption.

This regulation shall not apply to a dog accompanying any handicapped person who, by reason of his/her handicap, is physically unable to comply with the requirements of this division.

From:	City of Portland, Maine
Code of Ordinances
Animals and Fowl Chapter 5
Canine Waste Division 3
(revised 7-1-2009)

THE AMAZING BABY

The saying "ace in the hole," popularized in the early twentieth century, references stud poker where you're dealt a card face-down, which is called the hole card. If it's an ace, that's the best of all the cards and you immediately have an advantage over your opponents. Our "ace" on the original radio crew went by the handle, "Baby."

Baby and I both come from the world of boot-strappers. He's about fifteen years my junior. He and his twin brother Aaron are the youngest of five children, raised together in Lisbon, Maine. Baby hunts everything including pheasant and bear and is proficient with bow and arrow. When he goes deer hunting, he sits in a tree and waits. If war came to Maine, I'd want to be on Baby's side. He's hardy and hard-working. Built his own house, beautiful and big. One of those guys who can do things others cannot, both physically and budgetarily.

When we bought the old mill building in Biddeford in 2019, we needed to take down the corner that effectively abutted the river to create passage to the river walk. That is, take down what's called an "outside corner," where the corner of the building pointing outward turned into an "inside corner" facing into the building. The Saco River runs fiercely at this particular juncture, with active falls just above and below the mill, rushing over large rocks, creating lots of white water and spray and thunderous noise in front of our building. The only way the outside building corner could be removed was by parking a boom lift on land and hanging the bucket, the bucket in which Baby and Aaron would work, out over the rushing river.

Starting at the top, the two brothers removed the five-story wall, brick by brick, until the corner disappeared. Had either of them fallen into the river, he would have died. But if anyone could have navigated that churning river in work clothes and work boots, it was Baby and his brother Aaron.

RESCUING FLETCHER

In 2001, one of our original Radio Crew, Rico Suave, fainted in our office. Fishcakes took him to the hospital. Turns out he had life-threatening tuberculosis and was laid up in the hospital for a while. Not long after he went in, a few of us went to his apartment to check on his dog, a redbone hound named Fletcher. Baby's twin brother Aaron had returned home from the military in Southeast Asia with a female redbone hound dog that later delivered twelve pups. Fishcakes and I got a large male puppy named Cassius and a female named Bella, the runt of the litter. Rico got a boy he named Fletcher after the Chevy Chase character, Fletch.

Fletcher was a big, strong dog and a ton of fun, and when we got to Rico's place, he was very happy to see us. He'd been chewing on the couch cushions, ripping through the faux leather and pulling out the stuffing. It looked like he hadn't been outside in a while: dog feces lay about the floor in the living room, along with beer cans tossed all around on the remaining floor. Baby and a few others filled eleven large contractor bags full of the cans. Then Baby took Fletcher home. They were a great pair.

WHAT SOMETHING CAN BE

My friend Woody, married to Cherry, both of the original Radio Crew, is one of the smartest people I've met. He's quick and funny and adventurous and takes risks. I saw him flip over his handlebars once on a trail in the Pownal Woods, land on his back, and get up and laugh. Another time Judy and I saw him raise multiple, tall roof joists by himself and build the roof again by himself.

I don't know if Woody did well as a student or not, but I'm pretty sure he went to college. He's that kind of bright, yes, but that's not the intelligence of which I write. Like many of us, for a good while I thought intelligence meant good grades, a high class-rank, and what college you got into. But as we get older and have more experiences and meet different types of people, we see that there are multiple forms of intelligence.

There is nothing Woody can't build. Particularly, as you might imagine, out of wood. What might look like a ruined home: broken steps, sagging porches, leaking roof, doors blown-off, he sees opportunity. He sees a fun project.

At some point, maybe twenty years ago, I saw him cut several pieces of wood all at seemingly different angles. He measured once and cut quick. Then he put them together just as quick. No instruction manual. No how-to book. He had vision. I watched in amazement. Never have I wanted to sit and observe someone work as much as I wanted to watch him. He has a sixth sense it seems. As smart as I might have thought I was with numbers, I knew I couldn't hold a candle to that type of intelligence.

It's nice to have friends smarter than you and better than you. There's a certain comfort in it.

Here's to

    Woody's

        Ever

            Useful

                Intelligence.

                    Cheers.

PICK UP YOUR TOYS

My brother-in-law Russel (Muscle), and my sister Jackie (Wenchy), newly arrived in Portland from San Francisco, became our grounds crew. Green Lantern let them use his small Nissan pick-up truck to run from building to building with their tools tossed in the truck bed. Green Lantern saw no problem with the fact that the passenger side door of his truck didn't open, since he drove alone. But Muscle's only option was to climb in and out of the window at each job site.

In 1998, after we bought 8-17 Burnham Street in South Portland—a forty-four-unit apartment complex—the front yard required mowing. Wenchy's job. One of the tenants had three small children and another on the way, and the kids' plastic toys were strewn about the lawn. Wenchy piled them up near the front stairs so she could mow.

The father of the children came out and yelled at her for piling his kids' toys too close to the stairs, a potential tripping hazard, he said, for his pregnant wife. Wenchy, a very hard worker with little patience for complaint said: "You mean to tell me these are your toys, and now you're mad at me for gathering them, which you should have done?"

They got into an exchange.

Later that night, the Radio Crew went out for drinks as we regularly did, and Blue, our leader, said to Wenchy: "I know technically you're one of the owners of Burnham Street along with your brothers and your father, but I got a call from a tenant complaining about his kids' toys and the bad attitude of the chick cutting the lawn. He said you were yelling at him."

"Oh shit, ok, I'm sorry. Don't tell my brother."

SHAWNEE PEAK

Shawn, our carpenter, could do it all. He chose the handle "Shawnee Peak" after the former name of Pleasant Mountain in Bridgton, north of Portland. When called on the two-way radio Shawn answered, "You've reached the power of the Peak! What can I do for you?"

Working on the exterior of 285 Brackett Street in the late fall of 1997, Mike and Shawn and I were up three stories high on some scaffolding we'd made out of nailed-together 2x4s so we could paint the corbels just below the roof. We were a bit frightened, but determined to finish the last part of the three-week project. On this day, it was cold and windy and getting darker, and we knew the rickety scaffolding wasn't meant to hold the weight of all three of us. Each time the wind hit, the scaffolding swayed.

Shawn yelled, "This is giving me flashbacks to 'Nam! PTSD!"

"Shawn," Mike said, "you weren't in 'Nam."

"That's true. But if I had been, this would be a flashback."

YOU'RE TOO FAT

Green Lantern is about ten years younger than me and one of those guys who to this day, thirty years since I met him, still looks in-shape, even if he's out of shape. Sinewy, with visible stomach muscles. Me, not so much, being of the shorter, slightly stouter framework. We both played ultimate frisbee.

He drew a cartoon of us once in which he held a frisbee, thin. And he drew me, short and fat and bald, but for one hair shooting up from the top of my head, and bespectacled, which I am. The bubble above my head read: "Hey Mike, can you teach me to play frisbee?"

The bubble above his head read: "No. You're too fat."

Green Lantern recently reminded me that when we were younger, we both commonly referred to our peers who did crazy, scary things, or plain old stupid stuff as being 'brain damaged.' We'd say, "That dude is brain damaged." A regular refrain in the 70s, 80s, and 90s. I told Green Lantern last month, heartfelt, how my brain injury and particularly my compromised equilibrium, makes my life sometimes difficult. He wasn't buying it.

"I've always thought you were brain damaged," he said. "I see no difference."

THE WORLD'S MOST FOREMOST BOY

In the summer of 1997, Blue, Cherry, Green Lantern and I played ultimate frisbee at a tournament in Ottawa, Canada—quite a haul, particularly with my car, a very old 3-Series BMW that cost me far more in repairs than what I'd paid for it, used. The car and its endless repairs depleted me of whatever money I had, so I decided if it required any more work, I'd be done with it.

Our team was good, but not good enough and we lost in the quarter finals. After the big tournament party Saturday night, we went back to our hotel with the intent to keep the party going. That's when we got a call. Green Lantern and I excused ourselves and went into the bedroom. Our good friend Shawn—the Peak—had been found at a truck stop in Connecticut.

I fell apart.

I said, "Mike, what do we do?"

He said, "Fake it till we make it."

I followed his lead and faked it all the next day. We drove home after the last game on Sunday, and somewhere in Canada, between Ottawa and Vermont, my car conked out. I pulled to the side and luckily, Cherry and a gang were ahead in their car and stopped. I took off my plates, emptied the glove compartment, left the car on the side of the road and jumped in theirs.

When I got home to Portland, my girlfriend had moved out and taken pretty much everything in the place, including the dog. My car was sitting somewhere in Canada, and most difficult and hardest to understand—Shawn had died.

Our friend would not be coming back.

We held a memorial for him in my backyard. Green Lantern spoke and was funny, as he often is, and we laughed. That helped.

Then Shawn's sister told us that as a kid, Shawn used to refer to himself as "the world's most foremost boy."

That has stuck with me.

A CALAMITOUS BLOW

A CALAMITOUS BLOW

"Stroke is a sudden, calamitous blow. The brain is pinched out from within. A blood clot or bleed in the brain's arteries cuts off oxygen to the brain's tissues, killing them. The most stricken of its victims end up mere shadows of who they once were…"

Norman Doidge, *The Brain That Changes Itself*

PTSD

Home from the hospital on New Year's Eve of 2021, I felt quite a lot of fear and anxiety. I've struggled through anxiety and depression most of my life, but this time it seemed exponentially intense. I worked hard to keep up with conversations and every day had some sort of sobbing. I feared a recurrence. Throughout the days, dizziness and fog-headedness consumed me like when you have a bad head cold. I couldn't wait for bedtime and often went to bed right after dinner around seven, so I could lay my head on my pillow to stop the dizziness.

I stressed a lot. Woke often throughout the night, panicking. My blood pressure jumped high. It didn't feel like me. I thought, man, this is PTSD. This is real.

The neurologist in Boston told me that I had to do something.

She said, "You are either going to meditate or you are going to medicate."

"I'll do both."

LOW SELF-WORTH

"Many vestibular patients struggle with disorientation, confusion and memory loss, as well as anxiety, depression, and isolation on a daily basis. This affects your identity and self-worth.

Talk therapy is a valuable resource when you are struggling with the challenges of coping with a vestibular disorder so you can develop self-compassion and acceptance."

Vestibular.org

DISTAL BASILAR ARTERY CLOT

Notes from visitation with Dr. P.
December 11, 2023

"Dr. P. reflected that Mr. Watson had a left vertebral artery dissection in December 2021 with distal basilar artery clot extending to the left posterior cerebellar and superior cerebellar arteries. He had a thrombectomy. There was evidence for right medial temporal lobe CVA and scattered bilateral cerebellar strokes with no evidence for a brainstem stroke."

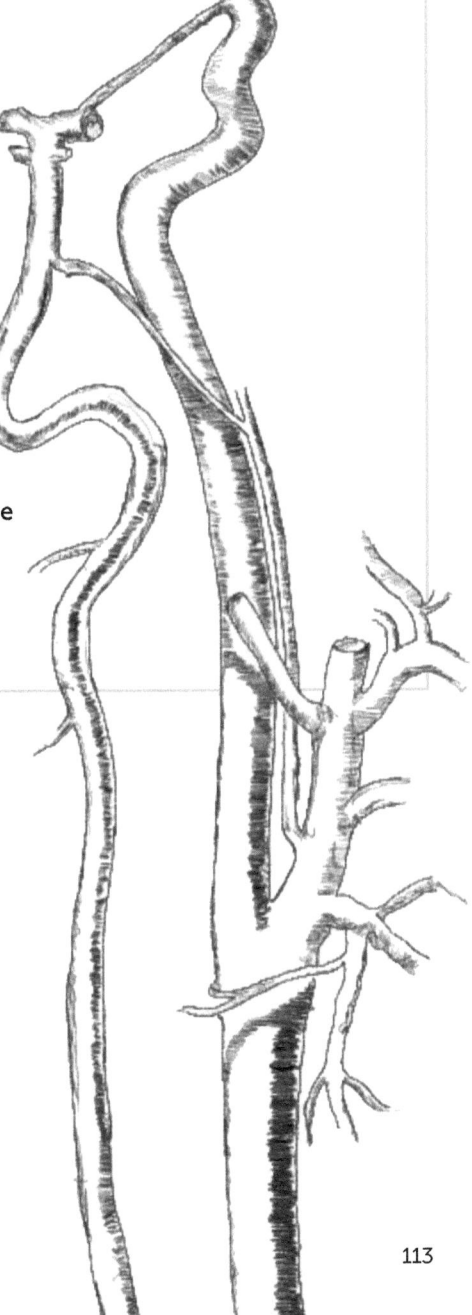

MIGHTY TIRED

I have seasonal allergies. Before the hit to my brain, they were manageable twice a year during shoulder seasons. Not now. Now allergies create brain fog. No cognitive issues, just a fully stuffed head and that creates a lightheadedness that throws me a bit off balance. My wobbly gait returns.

Cognitively, I can't keep up with conversations like I used to; my brain gets tired. Sometimes mighty tired. That's also in part because I'm managing nausea and lightheadedness every day.

I suppose it's a small price.

THE INVISIBLE INJURY

My brain injury is invisible. If I'd broken my arm, it would be in a cast, and you'd be aware that I hurt myself.

Not so with a brain injury.

When I returned to the office, many conversations went in-depth. I couldn't follow. I tried.

After a while, even though I didn't need to for balance, I began to put my hand on the wall and lean into it as though the wall kept me from toppling. This gave the impression to my co-workers that I was not so well. The conversations slowed down.

HOLD ONTO THE WALL

Certain things exacerbate the dizziness and lightheadedness. For example, a second glass of white wine, excitement, stress from work, financial issues, lengthy or involved conversations, being social. Most notably it's a bad night's sleep.

Doesn't happen often, not much at all, but when it does, I find the following day I have to hold on to the wall.

KEEP GOING

"If you're going through hell, keep going."

Winston Churchill

LONGER TO PROCESS

Notes from Neuropsychological re-evaluation
January 9, 2024

Language function: Expressive language was strong in informal conversation. He completed a task of auditory comprehension and functioning was intact. He took longer to process more complex phrases but completed all auditory requests correctly.

BACK TO THERAPY

In early 2024, after a nearly eighteen-month absence from physical therapy, it became apparent I needed to go back, largely due to balance issues. Judy and I decided, as well, following the advice of our insightful neuropsychologist, that I ought to enroll in occupational therapy since I struggled to type due to a weakened left hand. And given that every now and then I slurred certain words, saying dosh instead of dodge, and shession instead of session, I should also go to speech therapy.

You might think occupational therapy is pretty straightforward: I'm being trained to get stronger with things like holding a key between my thumb and forefinger, picking up coins, stringing beads, shuffling cards, catching a ball.

But it's not simple.

Nothing with the brain is simple.

Trying to get my left hand to move and act like my right, or to get it to move as it did before the stroke, takes an enormous amount of my brain power.

It's two things. It's strength. Working on it is like working out at the gym doing strength-work. Getting my fingers to do as my brain commands, and getting my brain to send appropriate commands to the appropriate finger is exhausting. Just trying to get my brain to lift my left pinky off the table while leaving the other four flat, tires me out. My brain needs a rest.

I've been given several exercises that work on both strength and dexterity. The most notable is called "Ok Shoot," where I lift my hand to shoulder-height, make an "ok" sign with my pointer finger and thumb, while the other three fingers point straight up, like in the NBA when they score a three-point shot. This is when I say "Ok." Then I drop the three fingers and turn my ok sign into a "gun" with the thumb as the trigger and the pointer finger the barrel, and yell "shoot."

Repeat.

Speech therapy is difficult. I can't say it's fun, though inevitably I crack up laughing. You would too.

I have to do tongue twisters like this one:

A tooter who tooted the flute tried to tutor two tutors to toot. Said the two to the tutor, "Is it harder to toot or to tutor two tooters to toot?"

YOU'RE SLURRING YOUR WORDS

"Betty's Butter"

Betty bought butter but the butter was bitter,

So Betty bought better butter

To make the bitter butter better.

YOU'RE SLURRING YOUR WORDS AGAIN

"Witch Watchers"

We supply wristwatches for witch-watchers

Watching witches

Washington wishes watched.

STRATEGIES

A number of vestibular disorders have to do with a malfunction of your inner ear, most notably the crystals in there. It's known as vertigo and dizziness, spinning. The medical acronym is BPPV—benign paroxysmal positional vertigo. For the decade and a half before the stroke, this is what I thought I went through maybe two or three times a year.

There's a procedure where you rotate your head once or twice, which is known as the Epley maneuver, that helps stop the spins. With Judy's assistance I'd done this a few times through the years. It didn't seem to work. Only after the stroke and having my brain scanned and seeing a multitude of black dots, did we realize that I did not have BPPV, but rather had experienced multiple mini-strokes or transient ischemic attacks, TIAs.

At occupational therapy at the New England Rehabilitation Hospital, the brilliant therapist A.C. and I agreed that my vestibular disorder is never going to go away. But we can develop strategies to minimize it. That's what I do with A.C., brain strategies.

ONE PEG AT A TIME

Pick a handful of coins out of the cup, put them on the table, pick them up and put them back in the cup.

Take this silly putty in your left hand and roll it with your fingers into the shape of a small ball. Then make it into a square.

Pick up one peg at a time, put it into a hole. Fill all the holes. Take the pegs out of the holes.

Here, shuffle this deck of cards.

Occupational therapy tires me out, not so much from anything physical, but from my brain working to connect with my fingers to pick up the penny.

FALLING DOWN

"Falling down

    Is part of life,

Getting

    Back

        Up

            Is

                Living."

José N. Harris

LIVE YOUR LIFE

I felt very lucky to have Dr. P. as my neurologist. Smart, good at what he does, scientific and realistic. He's semi-retired and shortly will be fully retired, which to him means lots more hiking in distant places.

Sometimes you get great life advice when you least expect it. In my first visit with him, I told him about my anxiety and my fear about doing a number of the things I used to do, like run, bike, and hike. Maybe I was looking for sympathy. Maybe understanding.

"Look," Dr. P. said, "at some point you've just got to live your life!"

Changed everything.

BETTER, STRONGER, FASTER

Growing up in Massachusetts in the 1970s, my brother and sister and I used to watch a weekly show called the "Six Million Dollar Man" about an astronaut who was re-built after a life-threatening crash: bionic arms, legs, and a left eye. He became super-human, spoiling the plots of multiple villains, many of whom were trying to steal nuclear warheads. He could outrun cars. The opening narration said: "We can rebuild him. We have the technology. We can make him better than he was. Better, stronger, faster."

All these years later, I now have the chance to be like Steve Austin, the re-built astronaut, and become *better, stronger, faster.*

Regardless of the fantasy, the only thing to do when you've been knocked down is to get up.

That's what I did.

SPIRALING UPWARD

Visitation with Dr. P.
December 11, 2023

Dr. P. told me that after a stroke some patients let the psychology become central to their being—that they focus on their diminishments, on having fewer abilities and reduced capabilities and dwell on the negative aspects of their impairments, and this can cause a downward spiral. This is not what he is after in his patients.

I didn't see it that way. Not once.

Slower to thought, tiring quickly, impaired balance, fingers that couldn't type, daily struggle with dizziness, so what? I was alive. People saved my life.

I was going to take advantage of this second chance. I was going for it.

Life suddenly felt like opportunity.

Dr. P. said to me, "I gotta tell you, Tom, you're doing great. You're spiraling upward."

KEEP RUNNING

The best way to describe how I feel with this brain injury is this: Imagine having a head cold where your head feels very full. That's it.

If you move your head quickly to the side, it seems like your head and your brain arrive to that side a second or two after you turned, eventually catching up to where your eyes are looking and where your nose is pointed.

To understand the levels of dizziness and nausea, keep imagining feeling that full head cold, and with your arms extending out past your side parallel to the ground, spin around. The more times you spin around, the more nauseous and dizzy you get. One or two or three time isn't so bad. When you get to five, you don't feel so good. Actually, you don't look so good either.

After walking the dog in the morning, it's as though I've spun around a couple times, a bit lightheaded. During physical therapy when I'm required to walk while looking up then down then side to side, it feels like I've spun about five spins, and I'm dizzy and somewhat nauseous. I like to take a break and collect myself before the next routine.

But I've been pushing myself physically—continually upping the ante: two miles, then three, then four, five, six, over the course of a month. I'm at the six-mile level now, albeit I travel slowly. It gives me that sense of spinning around a few times. So maybe I'm overdoing it at this point.

Maybe.

In any event, I'm wobbly and nauseous, and the nausea doesn't go away.

But I keep running.

AND RUNNING

"Run,

Forrest!

Run!"

Jenny Curran in *Forrest Gump*

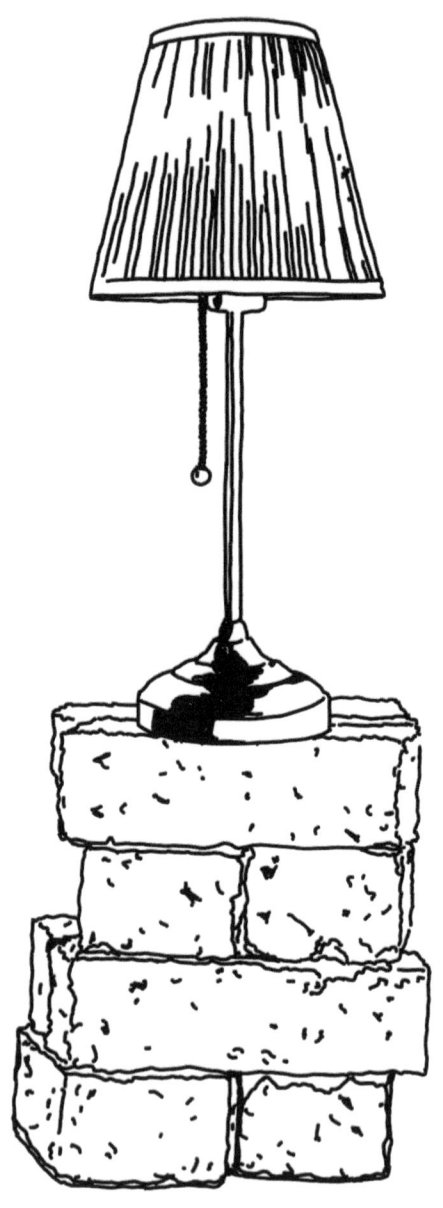

I LOVE LAMP

After the switch flipped, I thought, Who cares if I'm slow and tired, I'm alive! I survived a stroke.

In one pure moment of feeling alive, I blurted out loudly to Judy, "Man, I love life!"

For those of you familiar with Brick, the Steve Carrell character in Will Ferrell's movie *Anchorman*, you'll understand Judy's response when she replied, "I love lamp."

POST-TRAUMATIC GROWTH

"How human beings react to extreme adversity is normally distributed. On one end are the people who fell apart into PTSD, depression, and even suicide. In the middle are most people, who at first react with symptoms of depression and anxiety but within a month or so are, by physical and psychological measures, back where they were before the trauma. That is resilience.

"On the other end are people who show post-traumatic growth. They, too, first experience depression and anxiety, often exhibiting full blown PTSD, but within a year they are better off than they were before the trauma.

"These are the people of whom Fredrich Nietszche said, 'That which does not kill us makes us stronger.'"

"Building Resilience," Martin E.P. Seligman, *Harvard Business Review*

EMERGE

"By far the most critical skill… is what we call 'adaptive capacity.' This is, in essence, applied creativity—an almost magical ability to transcend adversity, with all its attendant stresses, and to emerge stronger than before. It's composed of two primary qualities: the ability to grasp context, and hardiness.

"The ability to grasp context implies an ability to weigh a welter of factors, ranging from how very different groups of people will interpret a gesture to being able to put a situation in perspective…

"Hardiness is just what it sounds like: the perseverance and toughness that enable people to emerge from devastating circumstances without losing hope.

"It is the combination of hardiness and ability to grasp context that, above all, allows a person to not only survive an ordeal, but to learn from it, and to emerge stronger, more engaged and more committed than ever."

"Crucibles of Leadership," Warren Bennis and Robert Thomas,
Harvard Business Review

SHOW UP

"We must walk into the arena, whatever it may be—a new relationship, an important meeting, our creative process, or a difficult family conversation—with courage and willingness to engage. Rather than sitting on the sidelines and hurling judgement and advice, we must dare to show up and let ourselves be seen. This is vulnerability. This is daring greatly."

Brené Brown, *Daring Greatly*

SHOOT THE PUCK RIGHT IN YOUR FACE

Most folks who play a professional sport tend to play to the very end, to the point where they just can't keep up anymore, and afterwards they're left without a career, just done with the old one. John, our CEO, had foresight.

He thought perhaps he shouldn't see his professional career to its natural end, but rather quit early and seek a second career. The problem you ran into was that if you were in your mid-thirties and all you'd ever done your whole life was play hockey, there weren't a lot of options for a next career.

He played four years at Boston University, the hockey equivalent of playing football at Alabama or basketball at Duke. After appearing in a couple games for the Colorado Avalanche, a storied, professional team, John needed more financial certainty for his young family, so he went to play in Europe for twelve years—mostly in Germany where his team won the country's championship and his jersey and number hang from the rafters of the arena he played in.

Between one of his last seasons, John and his wife Candace and their two children moved back to Maine where they were from. Prior to departing for another hockey season, John interviewed with several real estate folks in the Portland area, including me. We enjoyed our conversation and stayed in touch, and when he returned to Maine we talked again. At that time, I had no position available for someone who knew nothing about the business. I called my friend Joe, knowing he'd interviewed John as well, and said, "What do you do with this guy?"

Then I called John and told him, "Look, I'll pay you next to nothing. You can sit one office down from me and work and learn as much as you can."

In the five years John has been with our company, we've grown as much as we did in the previous twenty-five years.

Reveler.com

EATING ASBESTOS

There are many things that keep us from building the buildings I'd like to build or renovate. Zoning is a common one, where the rules allow a building to be only so tall and so wide, or maybe the building is too small to make it worth a go. You need size to achieve an economy of scale to make a project feasible.

Financing is another hurdle—partners and banks have to be interested in financial returns. Neighbors don't want a structure built near them. Bad soils can be too costly to remove. Any sort of environmental hazard is problematic. There's a general rule that if you're going to build residential, not to do it upon a former gas station or dry cleaner. Too much chemical hazard potential.

John and I, along with our financial partners, bought an old empty mill in Biddeford, Maine, in early 2020, which we'd wanted to convert to apartments. The buildings, two of them, were oddly configured, scaring off many would-be developers. We thought pretty simply that if the buildings were odd in layout, then so would the future apartments. Our architect and friend and partner, Ryan configured such apartments, and we were ready to go. But before we started building, we brought two of our partners through and one of them noticed a stiff, black layer of paper between the wood floor boards and the underlayment. He told us this contained asbestos.

And it was everywhere.

If it was asbestos, the project would die a quick death. Asbestos would be so expensive to remove that it would render the project financially infeasible. When you're this far in, that kind of news can be devastating. We brought the black paper back to our office and showed it to our construction consultant Mike.

He stuck it in his mouth, ate it, and said, "If that's asbestos, I'm dead, and I'm not dead."

HOLDING HANDS

After we won the bid to buy 82 Hanover in the West Bayside neighborhood, I told the city council and staff and neighbors exactly what I planned to do with the building—to make it an exciting retail and office and restaurant hub.

I knew what I wanted to do. I just had no idea how to do it.

I pulled together a number of smart folks who were some of the best at what they do: Mark of the Radio Crew, clever, scrappy, hard-working, and a master builder. Will, owner of Acorn Engineering and arguably the most experienced civil engineer in Southern Maine. And Mike, who knew all things construction, codes, and how to navigate the planning process.

At our initial meeting, I admitted that while I'd done a number of apartment building renovations, I'd never done a dilapidated brick and concrete garage. I said, "It's a bit intimidating. You all are going to have to hold my hand through this."

"We'll hold your hand," Will said.

We laughed.

Game on.

NOT POSSIBLE

When we bought the pigeon-infested, former city garage at 82 Hanover Street in 2018, Mike, our construction consultant, told me the price it would cost to do what we wanted to do—namely convert it to attractive offices, restaurants, and pubs—was way more than I'd planned on. At least twice, he said.

    Can't do that, Mike. Cost has to be x, not 2x.

    Not possible, Tom.

    Not an option, Mike.

    Not sure I can help you then, Tom.

    Don't worry about it, Mike. We got the ace in the hole.

    Ace in the hole?

    Baby. He can do it on our half-budget.

    What's Baby?

    Baby is Mark, our very own ace in the hole.

Throughout the lengthy job, Baby and I met regularly with Mike to review where we were until Baby finished on time and budget. Mike couldn't believe it could be done. For those of you in construction or in the building trades, you know the impossibility of completing a job at half-budget, cutting no corners.

That's Baby. Ace in the hole.

PANIC ATTACK

Were you to go to 82 Hanover Street today, you'd find forty-two thousand square feet of restaurants, breweries and barbeque. In the world of commercial real estate, most folks who invest with you want to know that you've secured commercial tenants (retail and office users) before you buy the building. Investors want to know you have a specific plan. But I had none with 82 Hanover.

Trying to raise the money for this project, while not a lot, proved difficult. Some longtime investors told me of their two halting concerns: 1, my area of expertise, if I had any at all, centered on apartments, not retail, and 2, having no specific plan and no pre-leasing could doom the project.

The latter concerned me too. There were very few retail, restaurant, or pub tenants in West Bayside—almost none. People didn't go to West Bayside for food and drink. In fact, most folks avoided it due to the multiple run-down properties, homelessness, and drug use. But for the very busy and popular Bayside Bowl, the area had effectively become a dead-zone. Who would come there?

82 Hanover smelled of oil and gasoline; the cement floor stained with mechanical fluids; the high wooden ceilings chipped and peeling of lead paint; the windows broken, pigeons making homes inside. On the pre-purchase walk-through, Baby and I both knew he could fix it and make it nice. But we hadn't bought it yet. Baby went home. I went home.

Given some of the negative responses from my long-term investment partners, and their lack of confidence in me, and seeing this place for what it was—a complete shithole—I'd begun to doubt the purchase.

I woke up that night. Sweating. Panicking. Heart-pounding. Scared.

Without investors, I could not buy this building.

Breathe. Baby, can do anything.

Wilsoncountybarbecue.com
Barpublica.com
Batsonriver.com
Argentabrewingcompany.com
Knickerbockergroup.com

Cyclebar.com
Exterus.net
Rfsengineering.com
Portpropmgt.com
Fortunetellertattoo.com

CONFIDENCE

"You gain strength, courage, and confidence by doing the thing which you think you cannot do."

Eleanor Roosevelt

MASSHOLES

117 Preble Street in West Bayside had been home to the Schlotterbeck & Foss Company, which makes great sauces and marinades, for over 150 years. They moved their operation to Westbrook, one town west of Portland, because it didn't make sense for them to rely so heavily on one freight elevator in their five-story building, when they could move to a large 1-story building with garage bays.

When we put it under contract in 2016, we walked through the food plant to check it out. My good friend and partner Joe and I were required to don hairnets, per company policy. I still have a picture of us in that garb. Joe is a handsome guy, maybe less so in a hairnet.

Our other friend and partner, John, led the project from purchase to financing to managing construction. Like me, John is a recovering Masshole. He and I verbally abuse each other, and this makes us very happy, even giddy, like two fourteen-year-olds.

That, in my opinion, is the definition of a Masshole.

We are proof that there are some things from which you never recover.

QUIET IN THE NOISE

A partner of mine once told me, "You know why developers have egos? Because they have to."

I understand the idea: real estate development is political and public, and so the developer has to stand firm and believe in himself/herself, and in the project. But the ego my partner references can generally come across as cockiness, which isn't a trait I admire or ascribe to.

Most of our projects get through the public process successfully, and I've noticed the steadiness that our two lead developers, John and Mike, exude through even the negative aspersions hurled at them.

A lot of noise.

These two seem to find quiet in the noise.

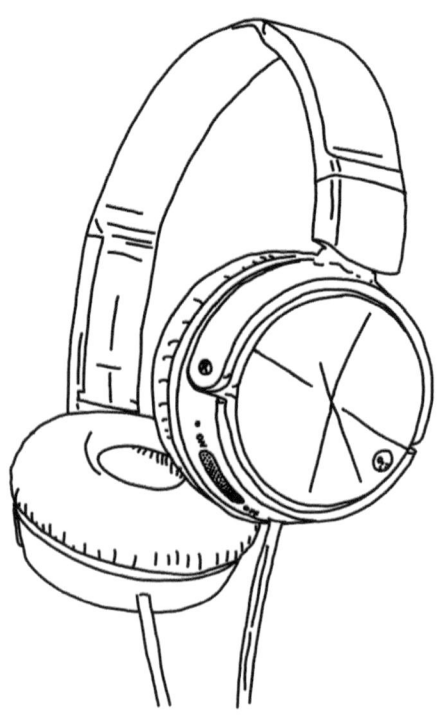

CARE LESS

I'm not like my co-workers. I tend to take the noise personally. That might be why they suggested I not go to anymore neighborhood meetings. I got mad easily, and it showed.

My friend Bill, our TD banker said, "Tom, you need to care less."

By removing myself, I found I came to care less. In part because my co-workers are so good at what they do. And in part because I decided to say "f— it," and it worked.

I found this liberating.

"TWO TEARS"

"Two tears in a bucket, mother-fuck it."

Lady Chablis in John Berendt's *Midnight in the Garden of Good and Evil*

A GLASS OF MAKER'S

John might tell you that I hired him so I'd have someone to drink bourbon with at the end of the day. That would not be correct, though that is how it turned out sometimes. There's something about having a glass with a co-worker that fosters truth and humor.

He and I talked a lot about real estate, where to build, what to build, and what the city might need. These topics got us fired up, and even more so over a glass. When the day is over and you are at the office, and you have time to breathe a little before heading home, this is your opportunity to reflect and imagine and to ideate.

In 2018, Portland put out what is known as an RFP, a request for proposals, to purchase six parcels in West Bayside. We won two parcels, 52 Hanover being one of them. But what to do with it? Sticking to our original plan of converting it to makers' spaces, became financially infeasible.

After a long day, John and I sat at our conference room table, each with a glass, to ponder the building's future. There seemed very few options for renovation—it was a building with eighteen garage bays and nothing else. What could we possibly put in that metal building?

Sip.

Then one of us thought, well, what if we razed the building and started from scratch?

What then?

Thearmatureportland.com

BIANCA SOLVES THE HOUSING CRISIS

In Portland, we have a substantial shortage of housing. A housing crisis. The solution is quite simple, but it would require public-private partnerships, which the city council, having enmity towards businesses, in particular developers, will not allow to take place.

Or they could talk to Bianca.

In the last ten years or so, Bianca has single-handedly added fifteen units to the city's housing stock without building any new building or using any vacant land. Apartments that before she arrived on the scene, did not exist. She is not a builder. She is not a developer. But Bianca has many talents, among them spatial awareness and a willful tenacity to make sense of the code department's cumbersome permitting process and scatter-shot documentation.

She got permitting to build six additional units in the basement of the Ambassador at 37 Casco Street, turning former maintenance shops into apartments. And at 707 Congress Street, a former first floor office into two apartments. If everyone who owns a building or is associated with a developer could do what Bianca does, our housing problem would be solved.

JENN'S PET BEDBUG

Most of us in the office at 104 Grant Street thought Jenn kept her bed bug in a small glass box on her desk to show tenants and coworkers what the tiny bug looked like in order to allay their fears of the blood-sucking mite. Not the case. This bug became her pet.

She checked on it daily. The bug had babies and they laid in the glass box too. Jenn found this very exciting and told many of us. I don't believe any of us returned the sentiment.

Jenn ran the property management company. I think her title might have been senior property manager. She was the boss.

I met her fifteen years ago when she bartended at the Skybox Bar and Grill on Brown Street in Westbrook. Sky owned the bar with her husband Al, who, during the day, drove a concrete pump truck to construction sites. Sky and Al are larger-than-life characters. Funny as funny gets. Smart. Quick. Wonderful people.

Everyone gets along with Sky, and Jenn was no exception. One night, most of the folks in our then small company were at the bar, celebrating a send-off of one of our employees. Jenn was behind the bar. She asked Sky if there might be a chance she could get a job with us. The next day Sky and Leyli interviewed and hired Jenn, her job being whatever they told her to do.

Jenn, like Sky, is a living success story. Back then she was married with four kids—two of her own, and two stepchildren. She later divorced and has been a single mom for most of her parenting life. She has a hard-working son, and an ambitious daughter at the University of Rhode Island. Jenn recently bought a house in South Portland, in which she does not have bed bugs. We believe her pet bed bug stayed behind.

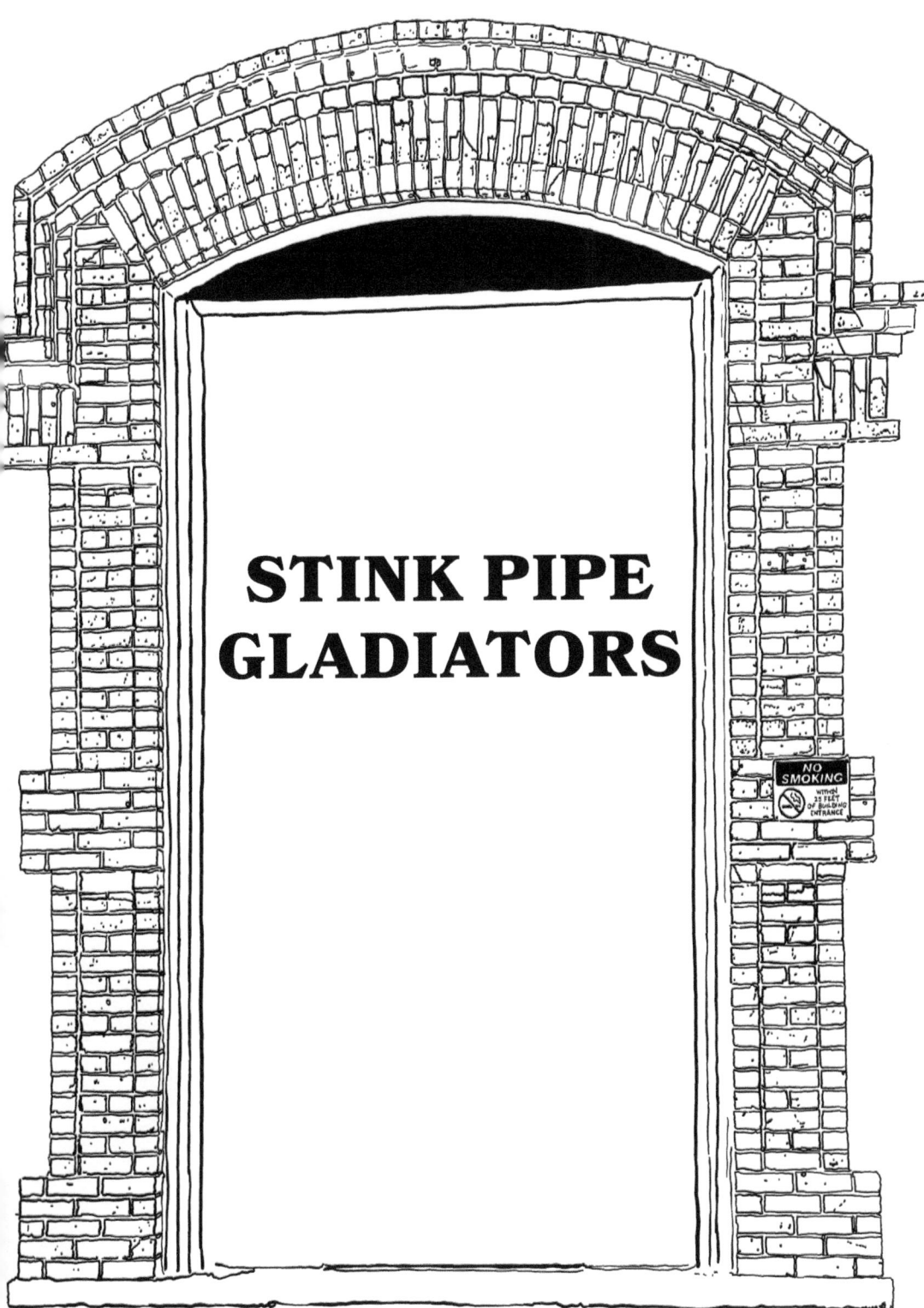

NO FEAR

"Fear doesn't shut you down—

It wakes you up."

Four says to Tris in *Divergent*

ONE MAN, 86 TOILETS

There are three of us: my younger sister Jackie, who's a chef; I am in the middle, a painter and sheet-rocker; and then there is my older brother John, the plumber who doesn't stop moving and doesn't stop thinking. He's strong. Very strong.

Around 2012, my dad, John A., and I, and a few investment partners bought the Lafayette, a 101-unit apartment building on the corner of Portland's Congress and Park Streets with nine storefront retail spaces. When a building is hemorrhaging water, it's almost always because of toilets, which often leak silently, unbeknownst to the user. I called my brother John for help.

Tenants will call you about a dripping faucet, showerhead, or tub spout, but rarely about a leaking toilet; mostly because that leak isn't too much of a nuisance to the tenant or it's so quiet it goes unnoticed. But the water bills are high when a lot of water comes in and out of your building like this, so high the bills look like mortgage payments.

Upon surveying every bathroom, John said eighty-six of the 120 toilets needed to be replaced with low flush toilets, and that he could do this in the span of three days.

And he did.

That is pretty much not humanly possible, which makes my brother not human.

There's an argument there.

To uncrate a new toilet (a toilet comes in two boxes, one for the tank and one for the bowl)—remove the old one, install the new one with all its parts and connections, and dispose of the old one—would take me, and most maintenance techs I know, about two hours to do.

John worked three, ten-hour days and finished. That means he installed and disposed of close to three toilets an hour, or one every twenty minutes.

No argument. My brother is not human.

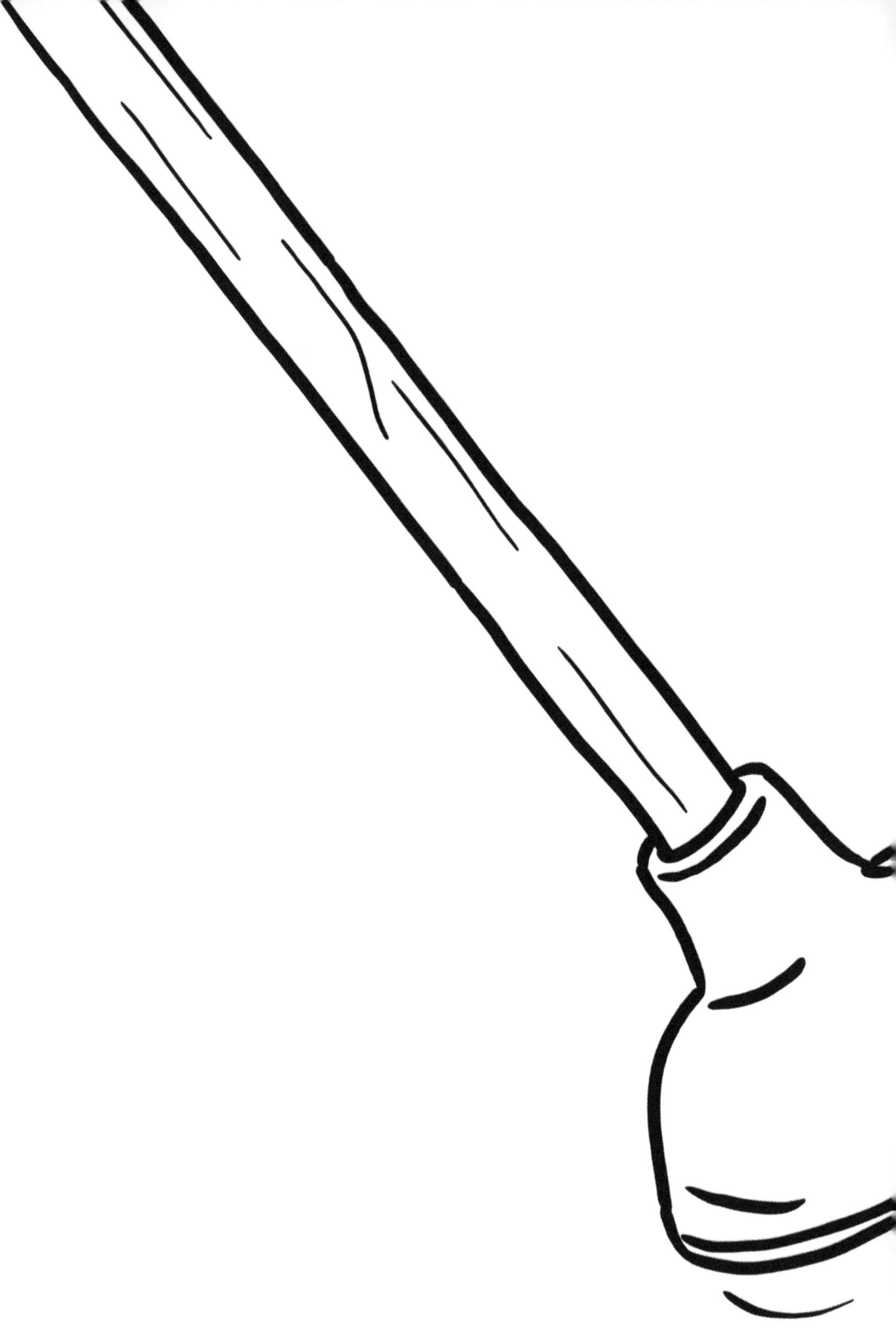

THE PLUMBER'S CREDO

John is a plumber. His son, my nephew Noah, is a plumber. They take that you're warm and have water very seriously. No matter what they have to do, or where they have to crawl to do it. In my opinion, plumbers are the hardest working tradesmen of all the tradesmen. They deal with all kinds of issues, heat, no heat, water, no water, backed up toilets, sinks and showers. They have to get into some of the most difficult areas, like attics, basements, crawl spaces, between walls, roofs. They have to lift heavy things, boilers, hot water heaters, pipes. In many cases they have to use flame or a welding torch in tight areas and so sometimes burn themselves. Same if they have to cut a pipe. They do so much with sharp tools that inevitably a finger, hand or arm gets a gouge.

Plumbers make sure your shit gets out of the house, and that you have water to drink.

Plumbers respond to emergencies.

Most tradesmen don't.

Not painters. Not carpenters. Even electricians will come the next day.

Plumbers will come at night. They'll come on the weekend.

Cut, burn, and bleed. (The plumbers' credo.)

IDIOTS, DIPSHITS, AND ASSHOLES

My sister-in-law, Ellen, who married my brother John, grew up in Hyde Park, Massachusetts, a borough of Boston. She's one of seven—three girls, four boys. They grew up in a three-bedroom ranch house, the girls, sharing one room, the boys another, the parents Frank and Eleanor the third. I dated her sister Kathy, played on a basketball team with her brother Billy, and have always enjoyed the family, one of the funniest.

Ellen and my brother John, the plumber, have four boys, now in their late twenties and early thirties, all living in Portland. John and Ellen live in York, about forty-five minutes south. Ellen, having six siblings, marrying a plumber, and having four boys, is a no bullshit person. Nothing gets past her, and you'll likely lose in negotiation with her. There is nothing she hasn't seen.

When I asked her of the key to life's success, she responded, in her thick Boston accent, "Well, like your brother says—avoid idiots, dipshits, and assholes."

ONE MAN, 120 RADIATORS

In the fall of 2005, after a few years of owning the Metropolitan, it became apparent we had too many radiators not producing heat. There were over 120 in the building, and each one of them had a steam trap which sits off the base of the radiator along the pipe where the steam comes in. The steam trap does just that—traps the steam in the radiator and doesn't let the steam out.

There's an enormous furnace in the basement that heats the water so hot it creates steam that travels up pipes to the radiators in the individual apartments. These radiators are large, heavy, of cast iron, and immovable. Every steam trap in the Metropolitan—every one—hadn't been replaced in decades and were malfunctioning or simply not working. My brother John replaced each one. No easy task, in large part because the cage in which the traps sat had rusted shut. He used all manner of wrenches, hammers, and saws to open the cages.

Leyli did the logistics, procuring the traps and cages and additional piping, and she made the operation as smooth as she could for tenants, which wasn't always easy with a 200-pound bald plumber yelling at a steam trap and hitting it over and over with a hammer.

EAT SHIT

At one point in the winter of 1995, three separate apartments at 286-288 State Street called me saying they couldn't flush their poop and that their bathtubs were backed up too. Turns out the apartments were in one corner of the building: one on the first floor, one directly above it on the second, and one directly above that on the third. I figured the stink pipe had clogged up. Not uncommon in the winter with snow and ice and various debris like old leaves, all of which together can clog the pipe on the roof.

The way a toilet works is that poop and pee and water go down the waste pipe, and air and gases go up what we call the stink pipe that comes out of the roof about a foot and a half. If that pipe is clogged at the top, air won't go up and poop won't go down. If you took a straw full of water and you kept your finger sealed over the top end, the water won't leave the straw.

But after an inspection of the roof, it became obvious the stink pipe wasn't blocked. That left me with the less intriguing and potentially nasty job of checking the waste pipe in the basement (your finger on the bottom of the straw, blocking drainage) where the poop and pee went on its way to the public street sewer line. This is a big pipe and has what's called a "clean-out," a big cap that can be wrenched off so as to see inside what might be going wrong.

I used a big wrench and some lubricant that I applied to the cap. No matter how hard I tried, I couldn't get the cap off. I opted to stop standing and got down on my knees for leverage and cranked it hard. It came off.

All the poop and pee and other hard things shot straight out into my face, a lot in my mouth, my nose, my eyes.

Problem solved.

Everybody's toilet worked.

TOILET BOWL HERO 1

First impressions, contrary to the popular myth, are malleable and easy to change. Great first impressions wane, bad first impressions improve. In Shakespeare's Henry IV Part One, King Henry sees his son, Hal, as a philanderer.

Hal spends much of his time in pubs with his sometimes friend, the "fast-witted" Falstaff, who's often found "sleeping upon benches after noon," tired from drink. The King, along with his cousins, is embroiled in a bloody civil war and all are unimpressed with the son. Their impression is that he's useless and will never be useful.

As the play progresses, Hal shuns his pub-crawling ways and goes into battle victoriously with his father, later to become the successful Henry V.

So it is that those men's first impressions of Hal were false. It's the same when someone's toilet is clogged. I'm hated. I'm seen as the reason for the clog, as one who hasn't taken proper care of the building.

I come over with my plunger and clear things up.

I am liked.

A toilet bowl hero.

TOILET BOWL HERO 2

"Say what you like

About Mr. Watson,

He acted like our kind of hero.

Stood there shining in the sun…"

Peter Matthiessen, *Killing Mr. Watson*

FIX MY TUB

In 1997, my dad and I bought a small apartment complex of fifty-eight units in seven, two-story brick buildings on Portland's Eastern Promenade, a beautiful area on Casco Bay with a park with walking trails, tennis courts, ball fields, boat launch, and beach. Though no one has confirmed it, the property, known as Macarthur Gardens, looks as though it had been built for military housing purposes, most likely in the 1940s. When we bought it, the property, badly neglected over the years, needed all kinds of repairs and improvements.

We renovated every apartment, every single one. Brought back the grounds, seeded grass, planted shrubs. We lined the parking lot. Put on new roofs. Installed new windows. This took a couple years. There were some super nice tenants who were encouraging and supportive of our work, glad to see the property owned now by a local guy and getting attention. There were also some really unfriendly and mean tenants. One particular tenant, a very tall and large and grumpy man owed two months of back rent.

I knocked on his door.

Big guy. Long beard, no shirt: You fix my tub, I'll pay you rent.

I fixed his tub.

He didn't pay his rent.

JACK OF ALL TRADES

The full saying as I remember it is "Jack of all trades, master of none," which is to say that back then I could do pretty much anything, just nothing very good. Even cleaning poop and pee out of the elevator took me two passes—paying tenants rightfully complained of residual smells after my first go-around.

A degree of self-doubt. How did I let someone pull his motorcycle into his apartment and take the engine apart on his entrance floor? How could I let pipes bang and clang so loudly for so long, upsetting so many, if not all, the building's occupants? How did I let someone get in our building to squat a lump of excrement on the elevator floor? (Note—it was the only elevator in the building, which was six stories tall).

These are not stories of success.

But if they're stories of failure, they're failures overcome.

HARLEY IN THE APARTMENT

Most basement units have direct street access—a door right to the sidewalk when a building is on grade, on a slope, and the unit is on the lower part of the hill, as is the case with two units at 288 State Street. The front doors of the apartments open directly on the Park Avenue sidewalk, right across from Deering Oaks Park. The sidewalk is wide, and the doors open inward as is the case with all entry doors—no concern that you'd swing your door into a passer-by.

When we were doing our pre-purchase inspection, I failed to look at the two basement units. We paid for them. I just forgot to check them out. Turns out one hadn't been lived in for years and had only exterior walls, rendering it a shell, with no interior walls or kitchen or bath. I spent a month re-creating it. The occupant in the neighboring basement apartment had wheeled his Harley Davidson off the street into his interior entryway where he'd taken much of it apart. It was not a small bike.

> You can't have that in here. You'll have to put it on the street.

> No.

> It can't stay here.

> It's staying here.

> It's a fire hazard.

> It's a motorcycle, not a fire pit.

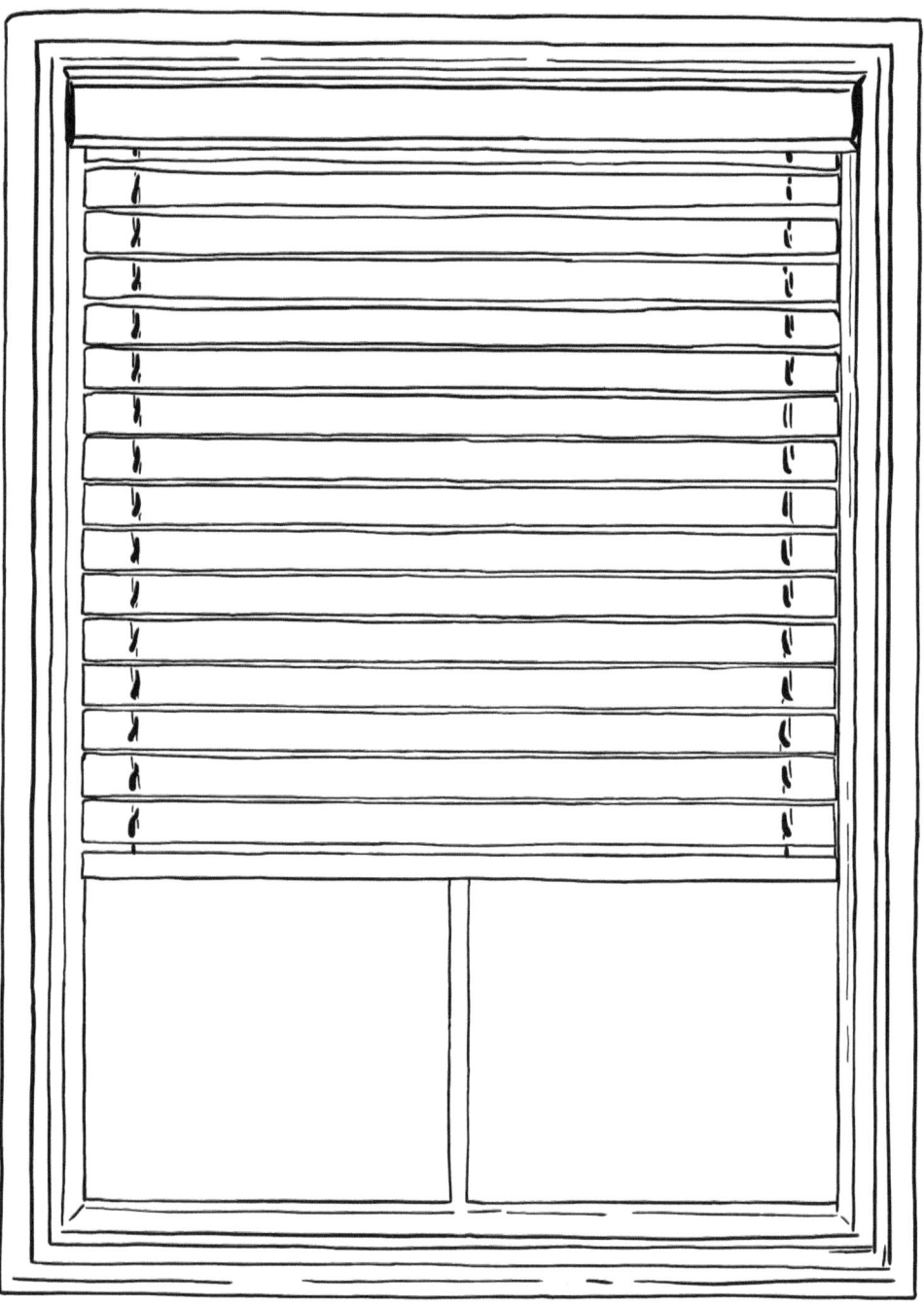

PULL THE SHADE NEXT TIME

Being a landlord or a property manager can be awkward. You're responsible for the peace, quiet, and safety of the tenants and the building. Every lease, which is the two-way contractual agreement between landlord and tenant reads in no uncertain terms that the tenant has the right to "quiet enjoyment." In short, the tenant has the right to live in his or her apartment peacefully and safely without disruption, noise, threats, etc.

As a landlord, we take this very seriously. Most issues, if not all, arise when a neighbor, a tenant, is in one way or another bothering a next-door neighbor, usually noise or smoke. While folks aren't allowed to smoke in our apartments, some still do. And noise is usually one of three things: the person next door is partying loudly with friends, or has cranked up the music, or is in an argument with his or her partner, all of which are not unreasonable until it begins to affect your neighbor.

We've found, over the years, people aren't in a hurry to call us about their neighbor being loud. Folks understandably don't want to rat anyone out. It's a tough position for a tenant to be in. As a landlord, we have to approach the offending tenant without revealing who called us. We remain on point, saying we've received complaints and could you reel it in.

Most folks do. Some don't.

Approaching or confronting anyone about his or her personal behavior is not a spot you want to be in. It's no fun.

Each corridor at our State Street building is double-loaded, meaning it has apartments on both sides of each corridor. The interior apartments, both those on the left side of 288 and those on the right side in 286, look into a central courtyard across from one another. I got a call from tenants on the interior 286 side. There had been an incident. Could I come over?

The tenants, two young women, explained to me that the man in the apartment directly across the way had been masturbating in the window and looking their way, and it scared them and worried them and angered them.

I knocked on the door of the apartment across the way. Then I sat down with the young man at his kitchen table and explained, you can't do that there. And you have to draw the shades.

He felt horrible.

He apologized.

I thanked the women for notifying me and told them it would not happen again.

PEEING IN THE ELEVATOR

At one point in the mid 2000s, someone peed in the elevator at the Metropolitan.

Peed in the elevator.

A tenant? A guest?

A puddle of smelly urine collected on the floor.

Motivation?

You couldn't wait until you got outside? Or up to the apartment?

Then it happened at the Wadsworth at 30 Preble Street, a sixty-two-unit building.

Again, the motivation?

I've had to pee bad in all kinds of places and circumstances, but it never drove me to that.

When we bought the Lafayette, we found a tenant letting his friend into the building to sleep in the back stairwell. Stairwells, and certainly this one, don't have bathrooms. That didn't seem to bother this guy. He pooped on the lower landing. Leaving it for us.

Back to the Wadsworth: unrelated to feces, but troubling nonetheless, a tenant on one of the top floors repeatedly shot BBs out his window in full view at the windows of the public market across the street where the police were parked.

Motivation?

THIS IS NOT FLORIDA STATE UNIVERSITY

The abbreviation for Florida State University in Tallahassee is FSU. In the mid-1990s in Portland, a gang of young men, mostly white, adorned themselves in Florida State regalia, most notably emblazoned baseball caps. The letters didn't, in their opinion, mean the university. It stood for, they would tell you, "fuck shit up." Which they did a fair amount of.

They wore backpacks which folks said contained guns, money, and drugs. Could have been T-shirts and underwear. No idea.

Many of them owned pitbulls, dogs I've found over the years to be playful and gentle. Not so with the FSU dogs. They were treated meanly, and they acted this way, barking, snarling, and leash bound with chain-like collars. The masters seemed to encourage this behavior towards people, not ever in my recollection trying to quiet the dogs.

None of the gang members lived in the buildings we owned, but they were friends or acquaintances with some of our tenants. At the entrances of 286 and 288 State Street, two columns on each side of the steps (I'm not sure I still like those columns today, but I guess I did at the time) support an ornamental cement awning. In the spring of 1995, I painted the columns a cream color, and my friend Mark painted the interior hallways a clean off-white. This brightened the halls, and along with the new carpet, made for a pleasant walk to your apartment door.

Next day I wanted to paint the cement awnings green and cream. I strapped the extension ladder onto my truck that morning to reach the awning. When I arrived early, around 7:30 am, I found the building had been tagged. The four columns I'd painted were adorned with big, red spray-painted letters: FSU. The brick exterior too, along both street fronts—State Street and Park Avenue—displayed their work with large and multiple, red spray-painted FSUs. The first-floor hallways that Mark had diligently painted the day before were ruined too, with punched-in holes and the same abbreviation, again in red paint, pretty much all over the walls.

There is a wonderful product called Kilz. It's a type of paint you get at the hardware store to cover things that normal paint can't. Most ink, pencil, and spray paint will bleed through a coat of latex paint no matter how many coats you apply. Kilz is what is referred to as a stain-blocking primer. It smells bad, the kind of smell that after five or ten minutes without a mask makes you feel high, maybe sick. I don't know what ingredients go into making Kilz; not oil and not water like most paints, because neither water nor paint thinner can clean the stuff off your brush. In fact, whatever brush or roller you use you throw out.

We painted the interior halls and the exterior columns with Kilz. Then put two coats of paint over that. Where FSU had tagged the exterior bricks, I used paint remover and a wire brush, and then washed them clean.

By the end of the day the building, inside and out, looked as it had the day before. No one tagged the building again.

DRUG DEAL

Best I can tell, most folks dealing drugs don't care who buys them or who uses them or what happens to users when they use them. Over the years, when buying multiple properties, I've met a number of drug dealers and had no problem with any one of them.

It's pretty easy to figure out who's dealing drugs. There's a lot of foot traffic to their door. No visitor actually enters their apartment: all hand-offs done at the door. Then after the exchange, the visitor is gone quickly.

My experience with the drug dealers I've met is they keep a low profile and tend to live alone and keep their place clean. They don't want to attract attention. Makes sense. Not so much because of what they do, but because of the rough foot traffic they attract, putting other tenants in a potentially dangerous position.

I've asked them all in-person individually over the years if they could please move out of the building in which they were residing. One particular young man attracted lots of folks, night and day, and these were not particularly nice folks, arguably quite sketchy. New tenants excited about their recently renovated apartment, very quickly began to worry about all the folks coming into the building.

For their sake and mine, I asked this young man if he would move. He said that since we were both businessmen, and we were now conducting business, what would he gain from this?

I wanted to tell him, well, I won't call the cops. But no, I didn't say that.

What are you thinking? I asked.

I don't pay rent this month and you pay the first month on the new place I get. Oh, and you have a pick-up truck—can you help me move?

He got a new place.

I paid his landlord.

I drove him to his apartment and moved him in, we shook hands, and he thanked me.

HIGH AND CLIMBING

279 Brackett Street had the reputation, among other things, of being a flop house. The top right apartment on the third floor—a small studio maybe just over 300-square feet where folks flopped, meaning where they administered their heroin and did what people do on heroin (which as far as I could ever tell wasn't much beyond zoning out) had six or seven mattresses covering the floor, perfect, I guess, for flopping. After knocking and announcing myself to no response, I opened the door to see a number of people sitting on the mattresses, most staring blankly.

Not that they heard me, but I told them they all needed to leave, which some did. The three that remained, I told to get out soon. No lease existed. No tenant rented the apartment. These were squatters. The drug dealer on the second floor on the other side of the building sold these folks the drugs they did in the flop apartment.

Late that afternoon, with the apartment empty of people, I changed the locks.

Next day, my brother and I unlocked the door to start our renovation. Three guys were sitting on mattresses.

Not possible.

The door hadn't been jimmied and I had the only key.

I asked them to leave, and they did.

Not until we'd been working in the apartment for a couple hours, did we notice the open window in the back corner, outside of which grew a tree with a limb extending directly to the window.

We cut off the limb.

ROBERTA

Roberta was my favorite tenant, hands-down. I don't know her life story, but it couldn't have been easy. I chatted with her often. She occupied an apartment—a room—on the second floor in the middle of the 279 Brackett Street building, where she had a guitar and a blanket. That's it. No bed, no chair, no bureau, no towel, no pots, pans, dishes, nothing.

She might have been ten years my senior. She put on very bright red lipstick and wore a tie around her short hair as a headband. The tail of the tie ran down her shoulder or back. She hung out during the day in Monument Square, and happily vacated her apartment when I went to renovate it.

"I'm outta here, brotha. I'll see you around," she said to me.

At one point, a few years later, I ran into her in Monument Square. She asked, "Still kickin' ass, Tommy brotha?"

Last I saw her, maybe before COVID, a cabby dropped her off with her bags of groceries at her apartment on Cumberland Avenue across from the high school.

I helped her carry the bags up to her second floor apartment.

"Yah, brotha Tommy, still kickin' ass."

ROUGH CROWD

My dad and I bought 279 Brackett Street in the mid 1990s: a fourteen-unit apartment building on the corner of Neal and Brackett Streets in the West End. Every part of it gross or in disrepair, often both: bad lighting, no smoke detectors, nasty carpeting, pervasive cat urine smell, cabinetry without doors, faulty locks on apartment doors, clanging heat pipes, broken toilets, malfunctioning windows, apartments that looked more like single rooms with a toilet. A rough crowd lived there.

A guy came by to purchase heroin from the drug dealer on the second floor on the left. I shooed him away. He pulled a knife on me.

My brother got in his face and told him to get the f— out.

He sat across the street, and the dealer met him there.

SOGGY MEAT

In the spring of 1995, after my dad and I bought two beautiful brick buildings on Congress Street (760-762 and 764-766) with slate mansard roofs, one door away from the Bramhall Fire Station, a tenant skipped out when the electric company shut off the electricity. He hadn't paid his bills. Like everything else in the apartment that required electricity, the refrigerator sat idle, and apparently shut off for over a month.

When I opened the freezer door, a smelly amorphous reddish-purple blob dripped out. Melted meat.

I did not throw up.

Close.

MASTER OF NONE

Upon receiving a problem call, when you're a landlord or a maintenance tech, you like to check it out yourself and triage it before calling in the skilled tradesman who no doubt will get it fixed and also be costly. The problem I've found is that I tend to take the triage a little too far; meaning, I dig into the problem and keep digging and get so deep and so far along that I decide to fix the problem myself.

This is not a mistake, though you can find yourself struggling. Particularly if it's a plumbing problem. In Portland, there's a hardware store on St. John Street called Maine Hardware where historically they've hired experts of all trades. I have a pretty straightforward M.O. with any plumbing issue: turn the water off at the source, rip out the offending part, usually a water pipe or some sort of drain, and bring it down to Maine Hardware where one of the guys finds an exact replacement part along with all the necessary supplies: couplings, glues, Teflon tape.

For the most part, I never know fully how to solve any maintenance issue, which is never much of a problem, since the Maine Hardware guys are so instructive.

Except when they're closed.

UNMISTAKABLE

Shortly after graduating from college, I moved back to Boston and started a painting company that morphed into a painting and sheetrock company with my partner Jonathan Adams. We called it Adams Watson. We liked each other and liked what we did.

We beautified the baths and kitchens where the plumbers, electricians, and carpenters put in so much effort. The smell of paint is unmistakable—fresh, clean, chemical, acrid. The smell signaled the finishing touch to all the other work that had occurred on the site. We were their finishing touch. We brought their work to life.

There are many different types of paint, and paint sheens, and chemical make-up. Back then, we painted the ceilings white, flat, no sheen, the walls eggshell (some sheen), and the wood trim, the doors, windows and the frames around them, the baseboard, and ceiling molding in semi-gloss or full gloss, usually a different color from the walls so they stood out.

The ceiling and wall paints were latex, meaning they were water-based and you could clean your brushes in the sink or tub. For the trim we used oil-based paint, and you had to clean your tools in a five-gallon bucket with turpentine, which smelled pungent and burned your nose hairs. This waste had to be specially discarded by an environmental hazard remediation company. Jonathan and I and the guys that worked for us owned two heavy canvas work bags full of various implements and all manner and sizes of brushes, sets for oil paints made of china-bristles, and sets for latex made of synthetic nylon and polyester.

We enjoyed our craft, and we were good at it. We often lost ourselves in it.

There is another side of painting, which is speed. You have to keep moving, the faster the better. On occasion, Jonathan and I raced each other, particularly if there were a bunch of panes to paint, like on French doors. I don't know that either of us won, maybe Jonathan, but this motivated us. We could paint the side of a French door in less than ten minutes and not get any paint on the glass. No tape.

HIGH AS A KITE

Water-based paints have come a long way and work well in almost any kind of application: on wood, drywall, flooring. They didn't many years ago. Oil set the industry standard: rich in color with a smooth brush-stroke application. It dried hard, much harder than latex, and was more durable. A lot of the older buildings on Portland's peninsula, the land between Route 295 and Casco Bay, have wide, sometimes ornate interior trim, and ceiling molding; the interior doors, closet doors, bedroom doors, and living room doors tend to have three or four "panels," giving texture to an otherwise flat surface. We painted the walls and ceilings with latex paint. But the trim we painted in oil.

Before environmental laws prohibited us doing so, we poured this thinner/oil-paint mess down the sewer drains on the street, which of course flowed to the rivers and oceans, killing fish and other aquatic animals. Oil paint and thinner created an awful lot of pollution and damage to the environment. Probably the main reason it's banned.

The Radio Crew enjoyed painting with oil because of its smooth application. In the winter, after a long day of painting trim, when we didn't open the windows, we found ourselves high as kites.

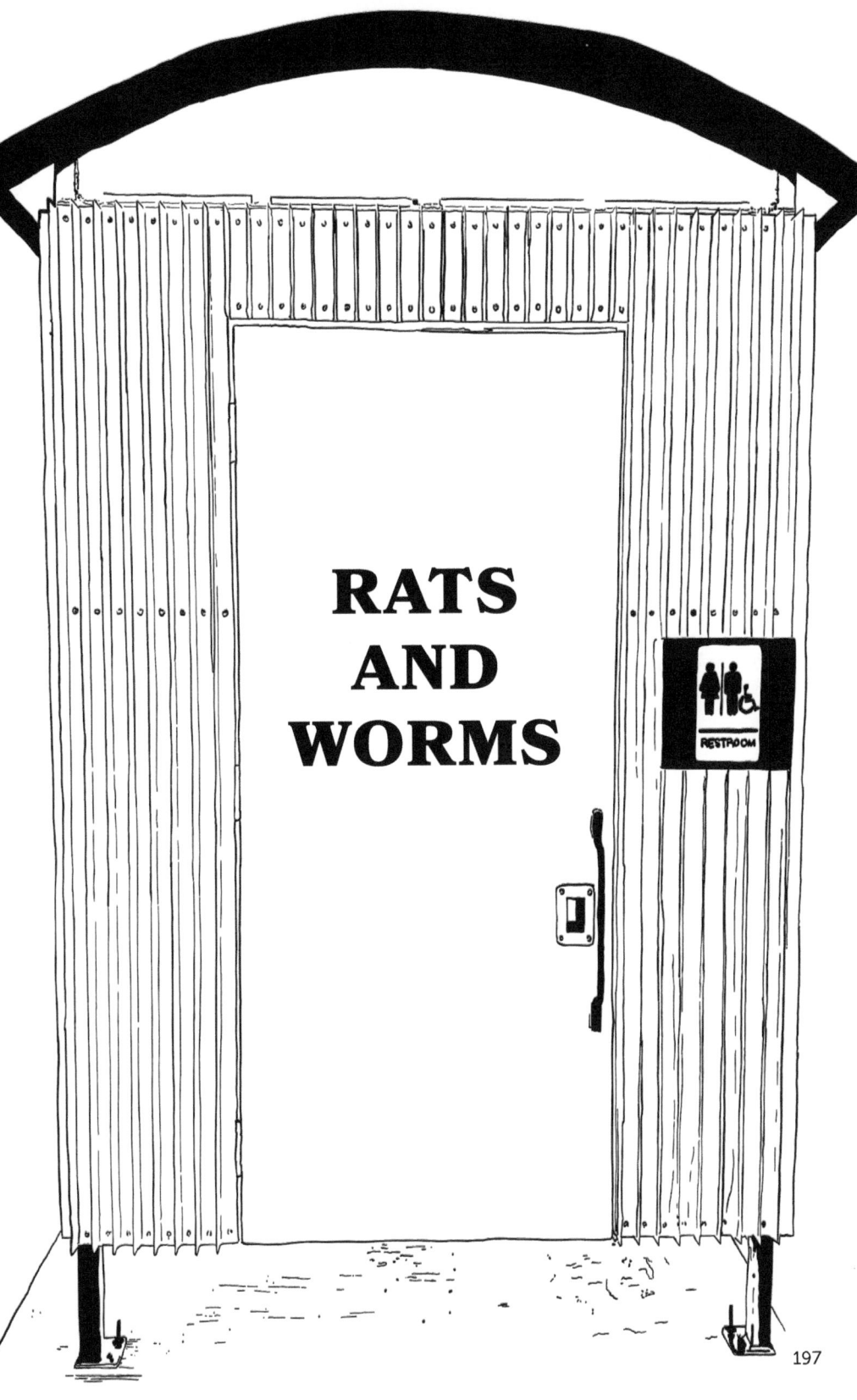

THIS ONE'S SPECIAL

In the 1990s, we used landlines and answering machines to which the landline phones connected and recorded incoming calls for later listening. I came home after work one night and Patrick had deleted most of the messages from our friends wanting to go out that evening. But he'd saved one.

This one's special. You gotta hear it.

> *Beep.*
>
> A woman screaming.
>
> *Shrill voice:* Please, please help me! There are ants in my apartment. And they're biting me!

APARTMENT B

Before cell phones, I used landlines to rent the apartments I renovated. After three or four days of renovation, I'd move to a different apartment in the same building and renovate that one. But landlines had to have a specific address: a specific house number or apartment number. The phone company demanded this arrangement; no exceptions.

It made no sense for me to put a phone line in any one apartment, given I'd be moving across the hall or up a flight or two within a few days. I told the phone company that I'd be living in "Apartment B" of the building, which meant the basement.

I asked if the tech could please put the phone jack and line in this apartment (that didn't exist and never would). The techs were good about bringing a line in from the nearest telephone pole and installing a jack in the basement, to which I connected a cord and a phone. I spent a lot of time down there, working on the boiler and the heat and the hot water.

All systems originate in the basement. While down there, I took calls from potential renters and asked them to come over and see the renovated apartment. For a number of years, I rented all the apartments this way. Each time I was in an apartment for a few days working on it, I'd run the phone cord from the jack up the side of the building, through the window, and connect the answering machine and phone and sit them on the floor. I came to understand that potential tenants who visited me on site and saw me working on what might be their future home—making it clean, safe, functional and attractive, wanted to rent from me on the spot.

Ring.

Come on over. I'm here now. I'll show you around.

BUILD IT AND BREAK IT APART

In the eighties and nineties, the oil used to heat your apartment sat stored in a 275-gallon oil tank that stood on four legs on the cement basement floor. At some point in the late nineties, the fire department made all the landlords encase their basement oil tanks within a cinder block corral. The logic being that should oil leak, it would be contained.

We built a lot of these and filled them with sand, per order of the PFD.

A few years later, the EPA and Maine DEP declared these enclosed tanks to be "underground tanks," meaning that if could you not see the underside of the tank, it would be designated as "underground," and so considered an environmental hazard; it had to be removed and disposed of properly with an environmental remediation company.

All those cinder block corrals painstakingly built per order of the PFD, we now broke apart with sledgehammers, then spent weeks getting the sand out of the basements into pickup trucks and off to the landfill. Then you could see the underside. No more underground tanks that were never underground.

THE UBIQUITOUS BUG

Somewhere between 2010 and 2015, bed bugs became ubiquitous. They were everywhere. As an apartment landlord or hotel operator, this was devastating. Where they came from, no one is sure, though the conversation pointed to the bugs perhaps having been brought to Portland from folks who'd been travelling from overseas.

Regardless where they came from, they were a scourge, and we did everything we could to eliminate them, but they stay dormant and hide between the walls where you cannot get at them. This is how they travel from one apartment to the next.

Like so many other landlords, tenants, and hotel operators, we were at a loss as to what to do. We started treating infestations like everybody else: with heat. An exterminator would set up a heater and blow very hot air into the apartment. Bed bugs, exposed to 118-degree heat will die in twenty minutes; the eggs require another seventy minutes.

While effective, it required an enormous amount of preparation on the tenant's part: removing items that could be damaged or altered from heat, like lipstick and certain foods; unplugging every appliance including the refrigerator; putting all clothes in a plastic bag to wash and dry them at a laundromat; opening all drawers to receive the heated air, and propping up the mattress so to get any bugs hiding there. Because the preparation disrupted your life, a number of tenants did not prep, rendering heating useless or damaging.

The exterminators would not heat an unprepared apartment. We had to, as the landlord, pay them nonetheless; $900 an occasion, heat or no heat.

We gave up on the heat treatments.

Leyli came up with some very practical solutions. If a tenant alerted us of visits from bedbugs at night—the only time they came out, and almost always went to the bed, biting the human, drawing blood, minimal, but still blood—Leyli gave the tenant a plastic mattress cover, trapping the bugs below, ending the nighttime biting. She also found that the bugs travelled from one unit to another through electric outlets to which she applied diatomaceous earth, the silica of which cut through the back of the bug and killed it.

In the end, Leyli won and the bugs lost. Three cheers to Leyli (again).

WE ARE THE DOG

The next thing we tried were exterminators with bedbug-detecting dogs to determine if the bugs were in an apartment. And if so, where? Apparently, these particular dogs could smell bed bugs unseen by the human eye since the bugs were hiding. The problem we ran into with the dogs is that we got too many false positives and too many false negatives, both of which were costly and not at all helpful to the tenant. A dog wouldn't smell bugs, and yet the tenant showed bites on his or her arm. We bailed out of using the dog-exterminators.

Leyli met some folks who treated bed bugs by cleaning upholstered furniture, carpets, and beds with steam and vacuum. This required no preparation other than to pick up clothes, wash them, and keep a relatively orderly apartment—putting stuff in its place. This steam cleaning worked great—and, bonus!—cleaned your furniture. This, coupled with Leyli's use of diatomaceous earth, began to eradicate the infestations.

Around this time, we changed pest control companies. The new guys called themselves Command Pest, and they were aggressive about their extermination. They told us that they used certain chemicals that worked instantly and effectively, and that because they were licensed, they had access to these chemicals while we did not.

> I asked one of those guys at Command, No heat?
>
> None.
>
> No dogs?
>
> We are the dog.

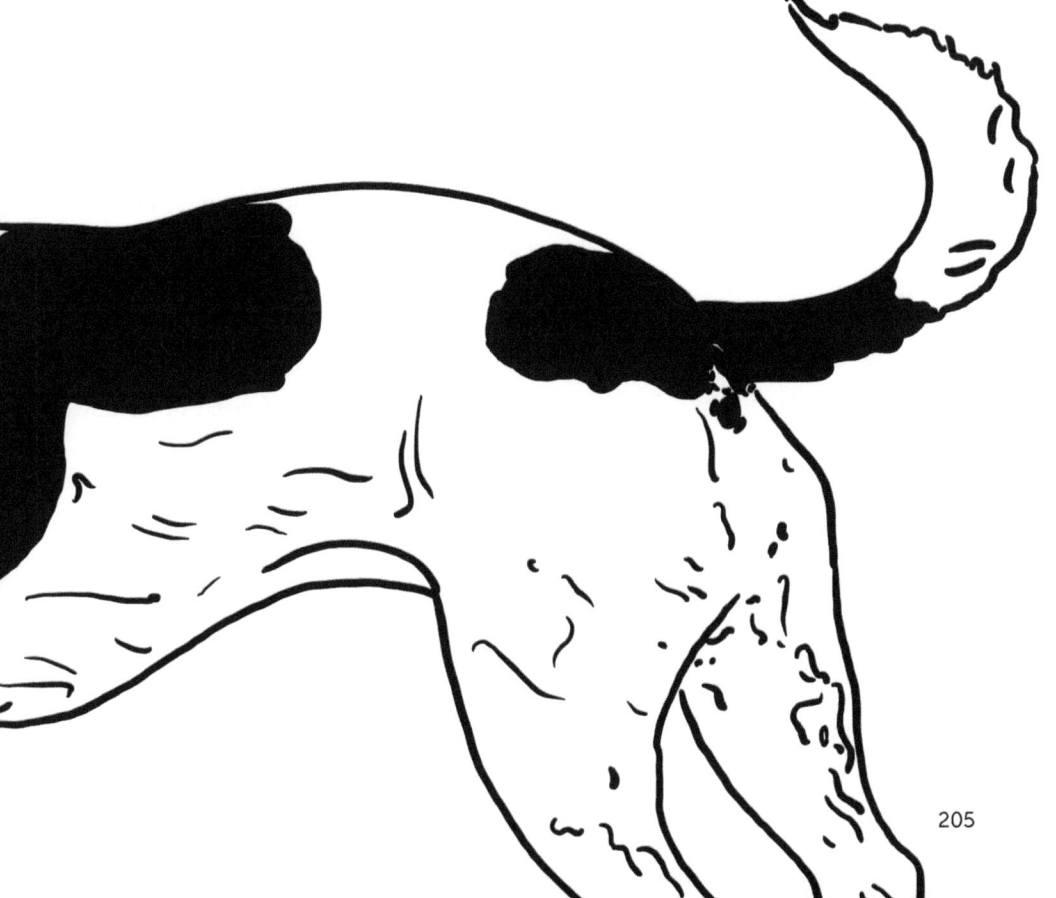

IT'S FREEZING IN HERE

Dude, it's freezing in here.

Commonly, when I got that call, I'd show up to be met at the apartment door by a guy in shorts, a T-shirt and no shoes in mid-February complaining that the heat hovered in the low seventy-degree range.

On this night, when I went to Pozzy's apartment, it was cold, too cold. Poz lived at 288 State Street, on the second floor in Apartment 7. During a snow or ice storm, the view out his windows into Deering Oaks Park took your breath away, particularly if ice had formed on the trees. The street and park lights made the branches glisten and sparkle. On this night, his radiators were cold, no warmth at all.

A steam system, at least the one at State Street, is what you call a one-pipe system. The steam rises through a pipe to warm up the radiator, and the consequent condensation drips back down the pipe to provide source water for the boiler. The radiators are big and heavy and made out of cast iron, and you can't move them. State Street has some of the biggest, heaviest radiators you have ever seen, sometimes with up to twelve sections, each weighing about fifty pounds. For the record, that's a 600-pound radiator. The heaviest refrigerator weighed half that.

In a steam system, the steam rises through a pipe usually on the left side of the radiator, connected by a valve at the floor level, that can be screwed up or down, moderating the steam flow, though most often it is left wide-open. On the very far right section, about four inches from the top on the side, is a small vent. On the assumption that the floor-level valve is wide open, it is the partial opening and closing of the vent that regulates the amount of steam coming into the radiator, effectively determining how full of steam the radiator will be and subsequently how hot it will become. Were you to take the vent off a working radiator, steam would rush to the radiator and out the now wide-open vent hole, unregulated—it would just pour out.

Pozzy's radiator stood stone cold in his big living room, even though the boiler was cranking steam into the rest of the building. The floor-level valve, opened wide, meant that valve worked. This then pointed to the side-vent as perhaps the problem, maybe stuck shut. I took it off to see if the steam would be drawn to the radiator with it wide open (having removed the vent, leaving an open hole). But it was a warm day for winter and the boiler shut off, sensing it had provided enough heat to the building, which got in the way of my experiment.

I went to the basement and turned the boiler on "auto," meaning it would run endlessly, regardless of its steam production, until I turned it back to its normal setting. Our office was situated in the basement just across the way from the boiler room, and the phone rang in there so I ran over to pick it up. The conversation went on for some time before I remembered I'd removed the vent on Pozzy's radiator.

I ran to the apartment, now thick with steam screaming out of the vent hole. My glasses fogged. I took them off, along with my shirt. I opened the windows and lodged the door open. Steam flew into the hall and set off the fire alarm system. The door closed behind me. I'd left the keys inside.

The fire department came.

I ran to the building's entrance to let the firemen know it was all okay, that I owned the building and that there'd been no fire, just excessive steam. Me—no shirt, soaking wet.

Please get out of our way.

I ran to the basement, turned off the boiler, grabbed an extra set of keys, ran to Pozzy's door and yelled, "Wait!" The firemen were about to kick in the door.

They allowed me to open it.

No fire.

A FIT OF EXUBERANCE

Every year, Judy throws a Superbowl party at our house that our neighborhood friends and our nephews—my brother's four grown boys—attend. It's always been a frolic, except when the Patriots play. Then it isn't— because the game always hangs in the balance. Most folks who don't live in New England hate the Patriots and their former legendary quarterback Tom Brady, who, in a span from 2002 to 2019, went to nine Superbowls and won six of them. No other team in the history of the sport has been that successful. They were a dynasty.

As a native New Englander, I loved watching the Patriots play, but our guests and I also found them nerve-wracking, largely because when they won, they won by very slim margins—squeaking out games in the final seconds. In the first six Superbowls, from 2002 to 2015, they won four of them and lost two, all by a margin of about three points. More often than not we celebrated at the end, preceded by nail-biting and too much nervous consumption of beer. We were, throughout the game, and particularly at the end, on the edge of our seats.

Of all the games the Patriots played, arguably the most stressful to watch was Superbowl 49, when they played the Seattle Seahawks in Arizona. The Patriots, tied at halftime, 14-14, seemed to fall apart quickly when Seattle came out strong and scored 10 points in the third quarter, putting themselves up, 24-14. The Patriots, as "the comeback kids" that they were, scored 14 points putting themselves in the lead, 28-24. With about two minutes left, Seattle began marching down the field, making it to the Patriot's one-yard line, threatening and likely to score and win the game.

But the Seahawks, instead of choosing to hand off the ball and charge it in, decided to throw a pass over the middle. It would end the game and Seattle would win if it their receiver caught the ball. He did not.

Malcolm Butler of the Patriots stepped in front of the Seattle receiver and intercepted the pass. The Patriots won. When Butler made that interception, sealing the Patriots Superbowl victory, we all went berserk.

Joyful pandemonium, hugs, chest bumps, beer spilled, maybe shots.

The next day, Monday, our property manager got a call from a young man, B—, a tenant living with his friends at one of our buildings. He told the property manager that in a surge of exuberance after Butler's interception, he tackled his closet bi-fold doors and ruined them and would pay us for replacing them.

I appreciated his candidness about his closet doors as much as I did his exuberance, an exuberance we clearly shared. I got him on the phone and thanked him for being so candid. We talked about the game. I told him we would fix the closet and absorb the cost.

PAINFUL STONES

In the spring of 2009, we bought 128 Grant Street, a six-unit apartment building on the southeast side of the street, between Deering Avenue and Mellen Street in Portland's Parkside neighborhood. For years our company's offices and maintenance shop were at 104 Grant Street (which is now twenty-three affordable condominiums built by my friend Todd). My dad and I owned 104 Grant and had partnered with Todd, who did all the work and developed the site.

Before the conversion of 104 Grant Street, and before we made it our office of many years, the low-slung building served as the home to Alice Dunn's Architectural Salvage, now in West Bayside, and before that it housed taxis and a taxi service. Just four doors down, at 128 Grant Street today, you'll see in the front, along the sidewalk, a low, concrete wall with a smooth, stone cap surface from which several vertical small stones stick up, making it very uncomfortable, maybe impossible, to sit on.

A number of young women used to live in this building, and on one occasion inebriated men drinking Natty's were sitting on the wall, cat-calling to a few of the women leaving the building. That's when I called the mason who cemented the vertical stones atop the wall.

The men stopped sitting there.

GOAT ROPERS

61-69 Grant Street was once owned by out-of-towners from New Jersey who decided to empty out the building by evicting all the tenants. The story became very public. With our office just a block away on Grant, we were interested in quieting things down, just not in that manner. While evicting everyone all at once might have been within the owner's legal rights, the idea of unhousing a group of people in one swift action like that seemed mean, thoughtless, and uncaring.

The property, four buildings, each containing six units, is not quite a block from Deering Oaks Park, and in the center of the park there's a wading pool that in various spots randomly shoots up streams of water—a place of refuge on the hottest summer days, a place my kids and I enjoyed very much. But Grant Street had historically been a tough street: crime, drugs, broken-down cars. And known to be the home of drug dealers, creating a lot of foot traffic and subsequent crimes.

The city and the police department once made the decision to put a community policing office on the corner of Grant and Mellen with the intent of giving folks a safe place to go if they needed police protection or help, and to make the police an integral part of the community. Officer Dan Knight policed the area. We got to know him and liked him. Grant Street quieted down after a few years. The office closed and Officer Knight now patrols Bayside near Preble Street Resource Center, a local nonprofit that helps all kinds of folks who are homeless, underfed, unhoused.

The owner of 61-69 Grant Street, prior to the out-of-towners, reclaimed the property from them through legal means. His name was Jeff, and I'd known him over the years to be a very hard worker. He'd moved to Florida a few years before and had very little interest in returning to Portland to take over a mostly empty apartment complex. In 2016, I offered that we'd buy it from him, as fast as possible, and he agreed.

Later, when I walked through the buildings with some of my co-workers, we found a number of used needles, lots of leftovers molding, and the apartments all pretty much ruined: doors off hinges, broken windows, kitchen cabinets without doors. The hallways and stairwells had become trip hazards with torn carpet and broken steps. The common areas smelled heavily of urine. My eyes burned. Plus, the buildings had no second way out, no second egress, which you need in order to be considered safe. Should a fire occur or creep up a stairwell as fire does, the second means of egress is your lifeline.

Were you to drive by the buildings today, you'd see large exterior staircases that provide a second way out. Our guy Mark (Baby) built them. Big, strong and durable. All twenty-four apartments on Grant Street also got new kitchens, new baths, and hardwood floors. Very nice people live there.

WATER HAMMER

In the first five years of being a landlord, I carried an emergency maintenance pager on my belt, 24/7. At night, I put it next to my pillow. One night, in the middle of winter, I got several pager calls from the same number. I don't know what pagers look like today or if they're even still in existence, but the one I owned measured half the size of a cell phone, with a tiny screen just big enough to show the phone number of a caller. No name. Just a number. Whenever the pager rang, it buzzed frantically and shook such that while it sat on a table, it would rattle and fall. (That's why I did not keep it on the bedside table, but instead next to my pillow. Not sure that made sense, either.)

I called the number on the pager:

Listen to that, listen to that, how do you like to be woken up in the middle of the night to that!?!

I could hear the loud banging on the phone. That's a hellish night, I thought. He lived in a basement apartment with steam pipes running along his ceiling. They were clanging. Plumbers call this "water hammer."

One of the ways the sound gets created is when steam travels up the pipes, and does so forcefully, just like it comes out the spout of a tea kettle and water is traveling down but somehow got stuck. The steam is trying to push through the water obstruction.

Big noise. Like a hammer hitting metal.

Rudy the plumber had installed that particular system, and I'd had him over once before to help me find where the problem came from. But when he came the system had made no noise, no hammering.

The tenant could see that I was trying to solve the problem, but with no success. I suggested it might be best that he move—that his apartment, due to the noise, seemed uninhabitable.

He moved.

A few months later, while ripping out walls in the adjacent apartment, I found, behind one wall, the problem. The former owner had built a second basement apartment, and in doing so had boxed in a heat return pipe (in which water is supposed to flow back to the boiler) between the new apartment wall and the outside wall. This was made of brick and stone, which gets very cold in the winter, and he did not insulate the pipe. The pipe, maybe a few months before, burst.

The water returning through it had frozen, expanded, and ripped a gash in the black metal pipe, preventing the forceful steam from going up and instead hammered at the pipe making a racket.

Rudy replaced the pipe.

I insulated it.

Quiet.

RATS AND WORMS

In 1998, before buying the Maine Wharf at 72 Commercial Street in Portland, now home now to the seafood restaurant Scales, I did my due diligence with my sea kayak and facemask to see under the wharf. There were so many pilings that at points I could not get my kayak through. Thick with pilings.

Other wharf owners told me the reason there were five to ten times the normal number of pilings under this wharf, was that seaworms had been eating away at the base of the pilings, and extra pilings were drilled into the sea bottom to keep ahead of the worms.

I couldn't see much looking underwater, the water being murky and with little sunlight. I pulled my kayak up to the dock and walked under the part of the wharf closest to the street, which could be accessed at low tide. The base of nearly every piling looked like an hourglass, large at the bottom, pencil-thin in the middle where the worms had eaten away at the wood, and then back to normal telephone pole-size above where the worms were eating. When you hear folks in Portland talk about a decaying waterfront, it's because of the worms.

Later, I stood under the front of the wharf, where at low tide the receding water meets the lower, rocky edge of land. This land, really a stretch of piled rocks, slopes upward toward the street, still under the wharf's street front building which is now the home of Rira, the Irish pub. I wanted to see the underneath of that upper part of the wharf.

I walked upward while ducking and leaning down as the floor of the wharf met the rocks. I think there were maybe two or three hundred rats scared by my approach. They scurried past me, under my legs. Fast. Into holes and under things and they were gone. Disappeared.

There are far more rats in this town than humans.

YOU SEE WHAT I SEE?

The Maine Wharf, like all wharves in Portland, starts at Commercial Street and reaches out into Casco Bay. Back in 1998, when we bought the property in which Rira and Flatbread now reside, the building stood vacant, a burnt-out shell. No walls. It sits adjacent to the Maine State Pier where the large, black and white and yellow ferries bring people to and from the multiple islands in the bay. You can watch the boats come and go, the travelers embarking and disembarking.

Numerous potential office tenants responded to our marketing efforts. I rejected the offers. I hoped that a restaurant or pub or coffee shop would find interest in the location, so that the public, including Judy and myself and our friends, could enjoy the space and the views and activity.

Many months into the project, a guy from Amesbury, Massachusetts, stopped by the wharf where I'd been removing loose and falling pipes from the first-floor ceiling. He introduced himself as the manager for Flatbread, a popular wood-fired oven pizza place. It sounded successful. A good business model. He went by Bobby and we had fun talking. He struck me not so much as a stuff-shirt business guy, but more of a surfer dude, which it turns out, he was.

We stood at the edge of the building where it meets the water. We watched a ferry come in.

You see what I see, Bobby?

Oh yeah, I see it.

Flatbreadcompany.com
Rira.com

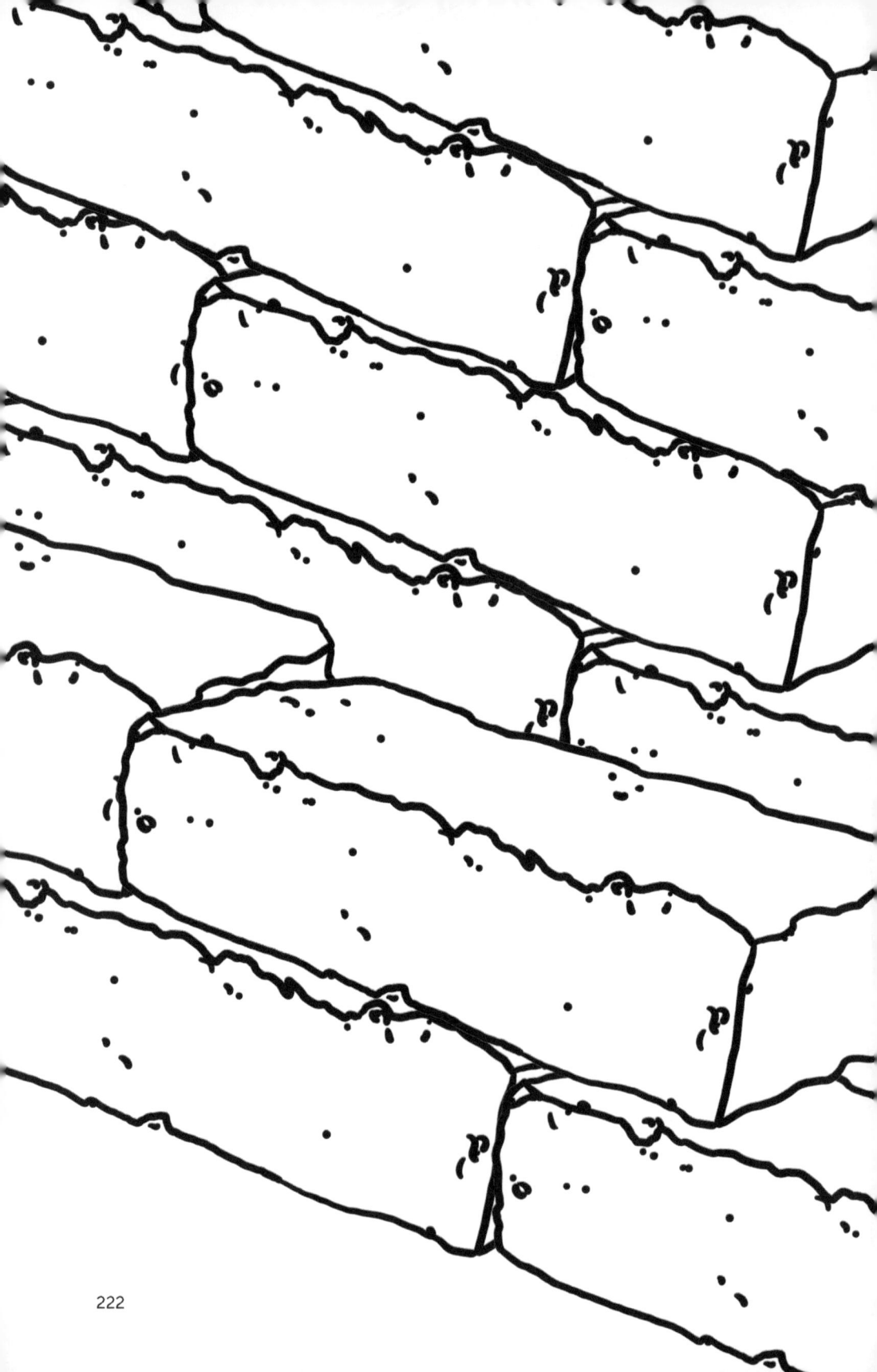

BRICKLAYERS

In the 1990s, Portland had an outsized blue-collar population—fishermen, lobsterman, sea urchin divers, and building tradesmen, carpenters, bricklayers, roofers, painters, plumbers. Most folks were from Portland, or at least from some close-by town. Back then, Green Lantern and I played in a cribbage tournament each Monday night at Gritty's. We arrived in our work clothes, splattered with joint-compound, caulking, and dried paint. We fit right in.

About twenty years later, to our surprise and maybe even shock, we found many people in town had impressive jobs and resumes. These people wanted new, modern apartments. Close to half came from "away," mostly from Boston and New York, as well as places getting too hot, like parts of Texas and Arizona. And the incomes—remember this is Maine, not a wealthy state—the incomes averaged well into the six digits, a lot of itinerant tech workers.

Our small city of Portland, Maine, had changed. And it wasn't going back.

It had been discovered.

BURST PIPE 1

Most of the residential buildings in Portland are three-story walk-ups, built in the early 1900s. In Boston we called them triple-deckers. They tend to be narrow in width, long in depth, made of wood with clapboard siding and flat roofs, and for a long time made of tar and gravel, though now of rubber. The buildings were comprised of three units, one on each floor. For the double-wide walk-up, there were six units, three on each side.

Each apartment consisted of about 1,200 square feet with two or three bedrooms that housed families with a number of children. Somewhere in the 1960s and 1970s, that demographic changed. Families began moving to the suburbs, in droves. This left the landlords renting to couples and sometimes singles. These apartments were too large for most of this smaller-sized demographic, and the landlords began to split these apartments into two. The landlord made more money renting two apartments as opposed to one, and the tenants paid less for the smaller space.

Just prior to this, in the late 1950s, hydronic heat (or forced hot water heat) came into vogue. No longer did you have to create steam in the basement boiler and send it to large radiators. Forced hot water heat starts like a steam system in a basement boiler, but you only have to heat the water to about 130 degrees, as opposed to boiling it to 212 degrees in the steam system. Small pumps, commonly ones you could hold in your hand, send the hot water into your apartment when you call for it by turning up the thermostat. That's the call for heat. Hot water circulates through pipes in the apartment—pipes wrapped by thin tin fins that radiate the heat. The fins and pipes are encased in light metal casings that run along the baseboard of the apartment. Hence the common name, "baseboard heat."

When landlords split the large apartments into two, they were forced to install new heat systems since some units would have been split such that they had no steam radiator, that radiator being in the unit of which it used to be part. Or the "new" apartment would have only one radiator, not adequate to heat it fully, not even close. Baseboard heat solved this problem, since you could run those hot water pipes pretty much anywhere you wanted to and several different smaller spaces.

The building owners in the 60s and 70s converted most of their buildings to the hydronic system. In order for them to get the heat to the tenants, pipes were run on outside walls, or above the ceiling but below the floor of the apartment above, through the uninsulated attic, sometimes in the entryway, sometimes the back stairs. Might not sound like it, but these were the shortest pathways. It should be noted that since the copper heat pipes were going to radiate heat into the tin fins, they were made with thinner walls than the ubiquitous copper pipes used for cold and hot water that is used at the sink and shower. The heat pipes, though copper, have a nearly thirty percent thinner wall.

This thinness, and the odd runs of these pipes, caused multiple problems. Water is the only element I'm aware of that expands when it freezes. Most things shrink. Water's the opposite. In the middle of winter in Maine, when it's towards zero degrees and the wind is blowing, the wind blows cold air into buildings, into houses, apartments; places other than doors and windows, though certainly those too. Basements, vestibules, entryways, attics, front and back stairwells can get cold.

A heat pipe just inside a door, perhaps running along the outside wall, is overcome with the wind and cold and will freeze up, causing a blockage, disallowing the hot water to get to the apartment no matter how high the thermostat is turned. And the apartment, without heat, and subject to the weather outside, gets cold, and we get the "no-heat" call.

Leyli and I often had to find where the heat pipes were hidden. We knew the former owners, and often several owners prior, had run these pipes with little knowledge of the effects of the outside weather, hydronics at the time being a new technology. Usually, the offending pipe travelled through an entryway or near an old basement window, and we knew if it felt cold to the touch, that was the spot at which it froze.

A heat gun is primarily used to strip paint off a wood surface. It looks like a hand-drill, and that's how you hold it; the end of it gets bright red-orange, and can heat at around 120 degrees. You can't use a blow torch on these blockages for fear of starting a fire, and a hair blower doesn't throw off enough heat. The heat gun works every time.

After each event, we insulated the pipes. Sometimes, no heat calls were worse than a blockage if the pipe burst. If a pipe froze and went undetected—let's say, for example, the tenant left for the weekend—the thin heat pipe would burst from the expanding ice inside. When a pipe bursts, the hot water trying to get through the blockage pours out of the pipe in a continual stream and ruins the apartment floor and the ceilings, and the floors and furniture of any apartments below. Usually, the tenant below called us about a ceiling leak.

Burst pipes are painful.

DON'T DO NOTHING

"The best way to

    Predict the future

        Is to

            Create it."

A. Lincoln

NOT IN MY BACKYARD

Once, at a surprise birthday party for a dear friend, a man asked me why we had a housing shortage in Portland and why developers and builders were not building more housing.

Three reasons, I told him.

First, the city has a rent control ordinance, so no one, no national or regional builder, will come to work in Portland, Maine. The pricing is government-controlled with no concern for costs, which is impossible to work with as a builder given all the risk and cost fluctuations.

Second, we have what's called an inclusionary zoning ordinance, which in Portland means that if you build an apartment building, twenty-five percent of your apartments have to be rented at a lower rate for people making under eighty percent of the area median income. It's a noble proposition, but it renders development financially infeasible when you consider that with current construction rates, it can cost over $300,000 to build a 600-square foot apartment.

Yes, it costs that much. (Think steel and concrete and copper wires.)

The third and last thing I told my new friend at the party, was that Portland was a place of multiple tight-knit neighborhoods, and that within them strong contingencies of residents didn't want something built near them. NIMBYism. This dissuades builders.

SQUALOR

Portland has gone from a good degree of squalor to boutiques, art galleries, restaurants, brew pubs, high-end homes, and high-end apartments. I have many friends, like my dear friend Malcolm, who liked Portland the way it was and lament the shiny place it has become. Malcolm and his wife Charlise live on Brackett Street, arguably on the edge of the West End, which has historically been a bit of a gritty street.

On the corner of Brackett and Pine is now a high-end apartment building with a high-end market on the street front, built about ten years ago. It used to be a vacant lot where neighborhood folks parked next to a decaying, crumbling single-family house with an exposed basement—a subterranean, open area where folks went to shoot up, just a half block from Malcolm's house.

He liked the simpleness of the town then. Behind his house there used to be a large, abandoned structure, sort of like a barn, with a roof caving in. Now it's fourteen high-end condos that my friend Todd built. Malcolm liked what it used to be, not what it is.

Malcolm is easy and he rolls with the changes, and maybe even occasionally does his shopping at the high-end market, but it's not his preference. Most people don't like change. Folks buy or rent a place for what it is, not what it might become. They like what they have. What they had. That's why they live there.

Until along comes a developer who's going to change all that.

OF MICE AND MEN

The hardest thing I've ever done—or that has befallen me—is losing peoples' money. By "people," I mean the folks who've invested with me; who've contributed their money to one of our projects.

We assess risk and we take it, and generally it pays off.

Sometimes it doesn't.

I don't mind if it doesn't and it's just me that loses. But even with my best efforts, the market can sometimes have a completely different outcome in mind; and when this outcome is so different than what we were shooting for, it can be painful.

If this happens—some big market shift—then I lose money, and in so doing lose other peoples' investment dollars. This is a hard reality to handle.

I don't sleep. I want to throw up.

It happened recently. It's been difficult for all of us. Some are angry. Angry at me. Some are in disbelief, wondering how this could have occurred. It went wrong, and it's painful.

Sometimes you lose.

Still, defeat, and in this case financial loss, sucks.

The Scottish poet Robert Burns in his poem "To a Mouse" is writing to a mouse whose residence in a farmhouse is demolished in December while the "fields laid bare an' waste:"

> "In proving foresight may be vain,
> The best laid schemes of mice an' men,
> Go aft astray,
> And leave us naught but grief an' pain
> And sorrow for promised joy."

Said differently:

> "Everybody has a plan until they get punched in the face."
>
> Mike Tyson

PROFIT

Profit is a four-letter word.

The fact is, neither I nor any of my developer/landlord friends would take on any project without the goal of making a profit. Far as I know, nobody works for nothing, and most folks would like to get paid as much as they can for what they do. If nothing else, it's a sense of pride; getting paid.

The difference between having a job and taking on a project is that the latter is full of financial risk and an ever-looming concern of failure and financial ruin. With years-long risk, comes financial reward. That's called profit.

Truth of the matter is it ought not to be called profit but rather margin, because for just about every dollar that comes to you, about ninety cents of it goes to others: vendors, laborers, the city (in the form of real estate taxes), and insurers. Your take is about ten cents. That's the margin. Ten percent. You can begin to see that if things do not go as planned, there's very little left for you. Sometimes nothing. Or worse.

I've owned multiple properties over the years where rents collected didn't cover the mortgage, and I found myself ponying up the balance, that is to say, out of my own pocket.

Negative margin.

Not a profit, a loss.

THE BROKEN WINDOW THEORY

Every summer on the corner of Caroll and Thomas Streets in my neighborhood, a beautiful, blue-angel hosta plant comes to life, but by mid-summer it's brown and lifeless well before its normal fall exit. This is because one dog pees on it. Then another comes along a few days later, sniffs it, smells urine, and pees on it.

This is repeated until the plant dies.

For those of you who are dog walkers, you know how this is.

The broken window theory is a theory of urban crime, vandalism, and decay, and it's much like the dog-pee-hosta case. The idea behind the theory is that if there are signs of urban decay, like broken windows gone unfixed, then further crime and vandalism will follow. Meaning other windows in the building will get smashed, graffiti will splatter the walls, and criminal behavior will ensue, like public drinking and drug use.

Recently a man named Russ stood across the street from my house, leading folks on a tour of the West End. The group collectively pointed at our house, and I invited them into the yard and asked Russ if I could give a brief, modern history.

I explained that our house, now sea-foam green with cream trim, had formerly been painted a very unfriendly dark brown twelve years ago, prior to our purchasing. And the yard was compacted dirt. There were no plants, and the front metal fence leaned inward, broken; the rails on the porch sagged. Russ told the group that in the 90s and early 2000s people did not come to Portland to visit—no cruise ships, no downtown hotels, no tour buses, no neighborhood tours. The group, seeing the beauty before them, found this hard to believe.

My neighbor once told me that in 2000, upon telling his father-in-law who resided in Boothbay that he and his wife were moving to Portland, his father-in law responded: "Why would you move to that shithole?!"

Much of the shift came about when many of us in town addressed the broken-window theory head-on. Not only windows but peeling paint: dark colors. Loose trim boards. Broken steps. Weeds. Dirt. Dog poop. Abandoned bicycles. Cars on jacks, no front wheel. Graffiti.

A good part of the beauty of Portland is its architecture, which for years went uncared for, in almost all the city's apartment buildings, inside and out. A number of landlords and tenants saw the potential and acted on it. Most landlords—not all, but many—got to cleaning up their properties. Some sold to more ambitious folks who had the interest and energy to repair and clean.

That's what we did. Repair. Clean. Paint. Make nice.

OUT OF MONEY AGAIN

If you're in real estate, you know that from time to time you run out of money. This has happened to me more than once in Portland, in large part because the buildings we own are old—most built in the first two decades of the twentieth century—and they require a lot of work. Usually more than we planned on, and more than we had the money to do.

In the West End in the early 90s, we owned several wood-clad apartment buildings, all of them with old leaky wooden windows. They all had storm windows to help keep out the cold, but we found the storms malfunctioned and were insufficient. Leyli and I were called often by tenants complaining about drafty windows. They needed replacing. Period. Hundreds of windows.

At a neighborhood meeting put on by the newly formed historic preservation office, the audience was told that within six months the West End would be declared an historic zone, and that any future projects would require their review and approval. This meant that all of our leaky windows would have to be replaced with wooden replicas, which at the time cost about five times that of vinyl windows. And the wooden window, being just a single pane of glass, would also require new storm windows to keep out the cold.

Vinyl windows had double panes, and as a result kept out the cold without needing assistance from a storm window. They were also a much faster and far less expensive installation. If you owned an apartment building, the future of our historic city became financially infeasible.

We contracted the next day with a window company, and in the next month replaced over 400 leaky windows. Tenants were thrilled, because no matter how warm your apartment is, if there's a draft coming to your shoulders from the window behind you as you sit on your couch, you're uncomfortable; you feel the chill.

That stopped.

We received no more calls from tenants about drafty windows.

SAY "UNCLE!"

In 2008, we bought 191 Pine Street, which sits on the corner of Pine and Chadwick Streets in the West End. We bought it as an apartment building with the intent to improve the systems and spaces, and sell them as condos—not our normal strategy. Our normal strategy being to buy older apartment buildings and improve them—maybe putting $25,000 per unit into each.

Turning 191 Pine into condominiums, would likely cost six-to-ten times that.

I hired my friend David to draw up the architectural plans and do the design work. But I had no precedence with this.

I got cold feet.

I called it quits.

I sold the property and David's plans to my friend Jason who did a fantastic job.

Sometimes you have to know to when to say "Uncle."

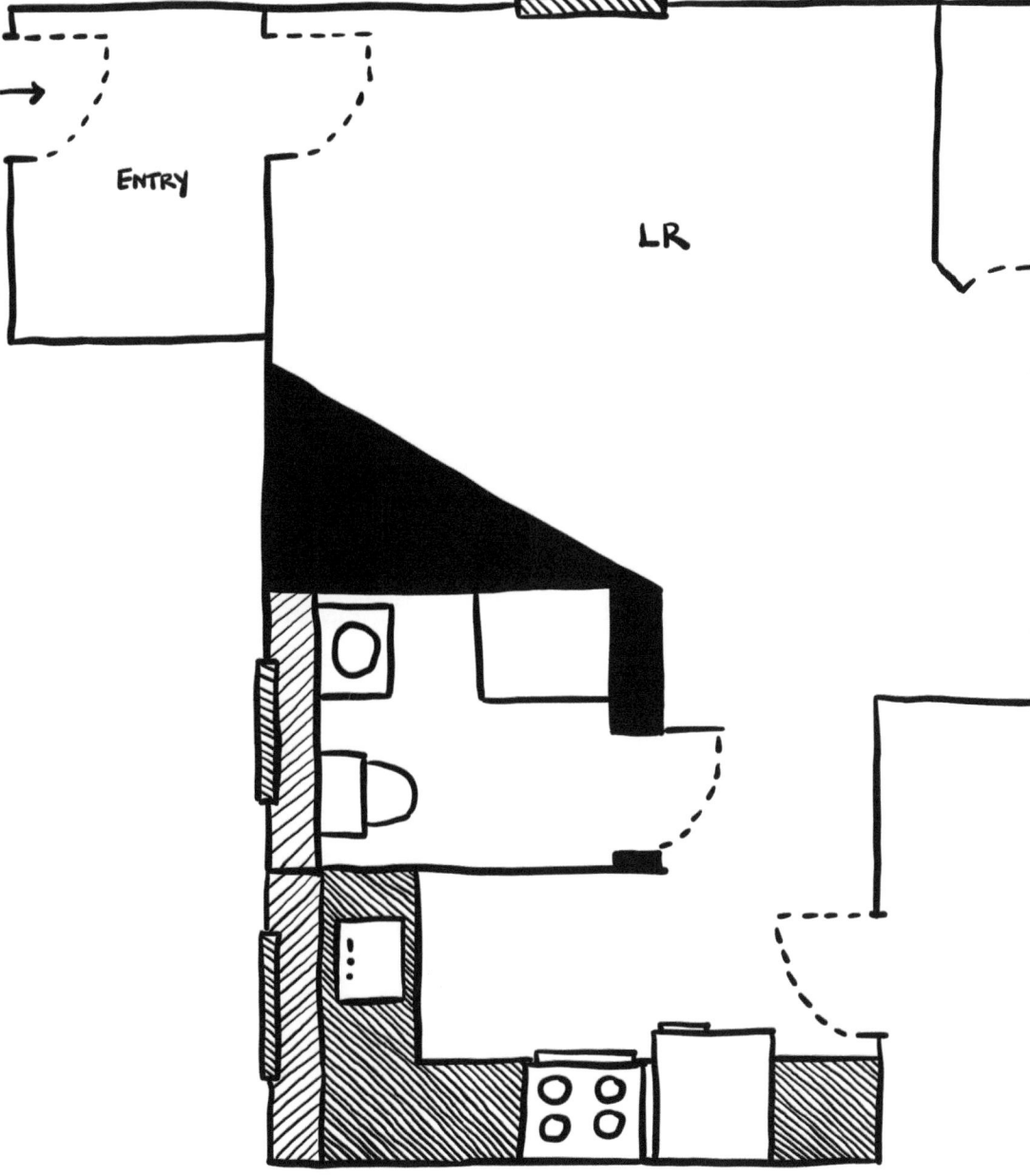

DAVID'S PORTLAND

Where do the walls go? How do you make them soundproof? How do you make sure there will be two ways out? Does the building have enough electrical capacity for new units? Enough water pressure to get up another flight? How do you heat the new spaces?

Someone introduced me to David.

David: Oh yeah, we can do this.

Our friendship began.

David is smart, insightful and creative. He's got a ton of experience—a master of architecture and building buildings. He can see things: how things could be, where others cannot. And he's tough.

David grew up in Natick, Massachusetts, about twenty miles from where I grew up in Acton. We're both Massholes. He served in Vietnam, then came back to Boston where he made his way through architecture school and started his own company in Portland. The city is full of his creations: large condominium projects, office buildings of glass and steel, street-level retail, brick historic renovations.

David's company, Archetype, is on Union Wharf, right on the water. If you know Portland, you've seen his creations. I don't believe any other person in the history of this city has so influenced and informed the way it looks and functions as has David.

Archetype has been in business as of this writing for forty-two years. The work he helped me with, the apartments he created and built, is small compared to all the other things he's done. David's my senior of about fifteen years, and he won't tell you this, but he knew I didn't know what I was doing at the start and that didn't keep him from working with me. His work is so complete. What input would I have? I knew best to shut up. He treated me like an equal from day one. Unbeknownst to him, he became a mentor to me.

I am lucky to have David in my life. The city of Portland is lucky.

GO AHEAD AND JUMP!

In 1984, the year according to George Orwell that we'd all sort of become automatons under the reign of Big Brother, the rock band Van Halen came out with a song called "Jump" that suggested doing just the opposite of the Orwellian tragedy; to instead go for it: take a leap into the unknown, into the future.

Take a chance of becoming who you want to become, who you might become.

Be independent. Be yourself. Jump.

I'm a strong proponent of "Go ahead and jump."

It's bold. It's courageous. It can sometimes get you in trouble. So what?

Recently, our son Sam stood on the railing of our porch, telling his mother he could jump over our wrought iron fence on the other side of the porch and land squarely on the sidewalk.

The metal fence is historic and has spearheads atop it, positioned for impaling. The jump, no doubt, would be an impressive feat.

Judy talked him down. No jumping.

When you start a business or change careers, or enter a new relationship, you're deciding to jump, to go for it.

Jumping is risking.

It's a "fortune favors the bold" move.

If you make an assessment and believe you can take the leap without deluding yourself, and you go for it—to me, that is courage.

Though to be sure, courage isn't always pain-free. You could impale yourself.

WHAT IT COULD BE

Joe, one of the brightest minds I've met, told me that real estate isn't what it is, it's what it could be. The Lafayette, at 638 Congress Street, is a good example of that. When we bought it in 2012, the enormous lobby sat empty, something folks quickly walked through from the front door on their way to the elevator. No one spent any time there, even though the windows on the Park Street side were large and provided streetscape views. Nobody seemed to care.

I asked our architect Ryan if he could draw the lobby as two spaces—retail on the window-side so that any store/pub/bar that rented it would get the streetscape views, and the lobby on the other side of a wall that we'd build with no windows, but had access to the elevator, which was exactly what the current residents used it for. Sagamore Hill, a very comfortable and well-appointed cocktail bar, took the retail space and fit it beautifully—this by two guys from Philadelphia who loved Portland and had vision executed on it.

Mark (aka Baby) did the work again. And he did a fantastic job.

Please go to Sagamore Hill, 150 Park Street, Portland.

Enjoy.

TAIL OF THE DOG

We're bigger than a small company now with about seventy employees and about 2,000 apartments in Portland, South Portland, and Biddeford, Maine, along with properties in Wilmington, North Carolina. But by big company standards, think of the ones you see in the news or drive by with thousands of employees; not us.

In our small sphere of the world, we might appear as the big dog. That is not the case. We are not the dog.

We are the tail.

We don't create the market.

We respond to the market.

The folks who create economic activity are those who create jobs. We rent to those people.

If we see a surge in the economy, and by that, I mean population-growth, and with that income-growth, we respond by building the type of multi-family apartments we think people will want, and can afford.

It's financial risk, yes.

Build it and will they come?

Still, we react to the market.

We don't create it.

We are the tail of the dog.

CAN I LEAVE NOW?

When we take over a property, most tenants are happy to have an attentive, helpful landlord. It is rare, and has only happened to us once, that existing tenants beg to get out of their lease. Usually, knowing we're going to renovate an apartment, we give the existing tenant ample time to find a new place to live. Sometimes we help with moving costs. Sometimes they moved into one of the renovated apartments.

At what is now called the Linden in Portland's Bayside neighborhood, a multitude of folks asked if we could please let them out of their lease, and we did.

Prior to our renovating the property in 2019, the property, owned by a college residential real estate group out of Chicago, advertised itself as a college dormitory named Bayside Village Apartments. Their online ad read: "Bayside Village Apartments are just minutes away from campus and offer USM, SMCC, and UNE students high-end features and A-list amenities at a great price."

This was not the case. And these students, maybe forty or so of them, requested to leave immediately.

Because the folks from whom we bought the building, as well as its two separate prior owners, couldn't attract students to rent the rooms, they rented to whomever they could. Different people rented bedrooms in quad apartments and didn't know who else lived with them. The bedroom doors in each apartment had their own dead bolt locks.

The building came to have a bad reputation. Police visits were common—there was a fair amount of drug dealing. A rough crowd lived there. Bed bug and cockroach infestations were everywhere. One tenant enjoyed riding his BMX bike down the hall, popping wheelies. Another tenant called us complaining a dog had pooped outside his apartment door. The videotape from the hall camera showed that his dog was the pooper.

All the young folks who wanted to leave immediately, we let leave.

MAKE IT DISAPPEAR

I can think of two occasions over the last decade or so where we had to shutter units, meaning close them down, get rid of the apartment. Each time, per order of the code office. This in a time of severe housing unit shortage. One made sense, sort of. One made no sense.

At 18 Casco Street on the corner of Casco and Shepley Streets, on the edge of what's known as Portland's Arts District, stands a sixty-two-unit, wait—sixty-one-unit, six-story apartment building known as the Shepley. When we bought it in the early 2000s, the basement apartment was trashed and vacant. We painted it, brought in all kinds of lighting to brighten it, installed flooring, a new kitchen, a new bath, fire door. The new tenant went on to live there for some time. But there was a problem, the Portland code officer told us, which had to do with the tenant's second means of egress. Its path travelled through the basement to the back stairwell, and measured just over seventy-five feet—too far a distance to be considered up to code.

We understood and suggested we build a reverse fire escape that he could access easily and use to climb up to the ground; now the tenant would have three possible ways out (the third being out his front door). The code officer said no. We asked the tenant to leave and shuttered the apartment.

Seems that in a city in a housing shortage, we could have come up with something to save that unit. Code officers enforce rules. They don't ideate.

Across the Fore River in South Portland on the Greenbelt Walkway—a seven-mile trail that travels along the marshy inlet Mill Cove—sit our Mill Company apartments: twenty-four houses, four apartments in each, totaling ninety-six apartments—wait, ninety-five.

The previous owner, a large real estate company out of Rochester, New York, had taken one of the first-floor, one-bedroom apartments and turned it into an office. We felt it should be what it had been, an apartment. We moved the office to the garage where we split the space in two: part of the garage would hold our building supplies, the other would be the office. We insulated the small space and put a heater in it. A door and two windows already existed, making the space light and easy to get in and out of.

Turning the former office back to its old self proved easy, since all they'd really done was put a desk and a copy machine in it. The bathroom and kitchen were exactly as they'd always been. We cleaned it and painted it, making it ready to rent. I went to the South Portland Code Department to let them know what we were doing—turning the apartment back into an apartment.

> No, they said, You can't do that. You can't add more units in a waterfront zone.

> But the apartment's already there. It's been there with all the other apartments since the 1940s.

> No, it's not an apartment. It's an office.

> The former owner put a desk in the apartment and called it an office.

> That's right. It's an office.

> I understand. I'd like to turn it back to its former self, to an apartment.

> No. You can't do that. You can't add more units in a waterfront zone.

Mill Company Apartments is a ninety-five-unit apartment complex. With one office.

HISTORICALLY SIGNIFICANT, MAYBE NOT

If you drive along Commercial Street, the southeast side has wharves and sea; the northwest side, the only side with buildings, is monotonously brick. Even the new buildings, of which several were built in the last few years—mostly hotels with street-level restaurants and bars, are of brick façade. Just this year, a new hotel opened in my neighborhood in the West End—the Longfellow— and it too is brick. Both these areas, the West End and Commercial Street, have been designated as historical neighborhoods, which means the city's historic preservation committee will only let you clad your new building in the same materials used about 125 years ago: brick.

There are so many wonderful exterior facades available. In the larger cities you see a lot of glass, especially on taller buildings. There are all kinds of metals and faux metals. Our 171-unit apartment building at 52 Hanover in West Bayside (not a historic district) is clad in metal. Hardy-plank, a light-cement clapboard, or shingled board that imitates the look of wood-siding, is attractive, strong, and keeps out the weather. Very popular across the country. Not allowed here in the historic zones.

HALF THE AMERICAN WORK FORCE

"In the first stages of hiring…If you [the employer] require a Bachelor's Degree [from job applicants] you lose out on half the American workforce. This systemically disadvantages candidates who acquire skills through alternative routes—at trade schools or two-year community colleges, through apprenticeships or military service, or by teaching themselves or learning on the job."

Adam Grant, *Hidden Potential*

BLUE COLLAR BRAINS

Over the last forty-years, I've watched different folks diagnose a mechanical problem using their brains, patience, and experience. Then there are folks who can imagine a whole new way of doing something. Out with the old, out with existing. In with the new, the inventive. My brother John is like this. He's a plumber. He's a lot of things. One thing for sure is that he's creative.

It so happens he applies his ingenuity primarily to water, heat and cooling. Truth is, he lives this ingenious life applying his insights to all sorts of physical puzzles and opportunities.

Most of the folks I work with, being in the management and operations of buildings and their systems, and this includes the envelope system—those parts of the buildings like roofs, windows, and siding that keep weather out—are inventive like my older brother.

Sometimes, particularly at night on an emergency call, you're left needing a part you can't get, no matter how prepared you are or how well stocked your truck is. But you've got to do something. This is where inventiveness comes in. It's cliché, yes, but necessity is the mother of invention.

I had the good fortune of working with some brilliant diagnostic minds, and all of them worked with their hands for a living. Some years ago, we hired a couple of very smart and affable brand managers, who were charged with figuring out what we did well, why we did what we did, and then rolling this into a brand, something by which you could define your company differently from others that do what you do.

These brand creators interviewed close to twenty of our employees to get an understanding of who we were and what made us tick. After assembling the data from the interviews, they brought to us their findings, one of which was their surprise at how smart the employees were, including the maintenance staff.

This is what I call white collar bias.

It's classism.

It's the tradesmem like the maintenance techs who keep us alive and well.

How would we do without heat in our Maine winters?

How would people in the south do without AC in the summer?

How would folks who work in offices do without fresh air?

Lighting. Water. Waste management. Roofs. Walls. Doors. Floors. Life safety-sprinkler systems, smoke detectors, ways out…

For some reason, people who went to college and got an office job think they're better—or smarter—than those who didn't go to college and became tradesmen.

They're wrong.

YOUR WORST ACT

If you've never been to Montgomery, Alabama, well, you need to go. If, like me, you're white and have lived mostly around white people, then to the extent I can insist, I insist you go. If your eyes are not open or haven't been opened to racial injustice in America, this will open them wide.

The Legacy Museum there tells the story of slavery and its continued legacy, and the National Memorial for Peace and Justice, also known as the Lynching Museum, will instill in you the terror Black Americans lived through well beyond the years of slavery.

The founder, Bryan Stevenson, authored the book *Just Mercy* about his work as an attorney defending, among many of the poor and wrongly condemned, those on death row awaiting execution.

This quote, among many in the book, stuck with me:

"We have abolished parole in many states. We have invented slogans like 'three strikes and you're out' to communicate our toughness. We've given up on rehabilitation, education, and services for the imprisoned because providing assistance to the incarcerated is apparently too kind and compassionate. We've institutionalized policies that reduce people to their worst acts and permanently label them 'criminal,' 'murderer,' 'rapist,' 'thief,' 'drug dealer,' 'sex offender,' and 'felon'—identities they cannot change regardless of the circumstances of their crimes or any improvements they might make in their lives.

"I've also represented people who have committed terrible crimes but nonetheless struggle to recover and to find redemption. I have discovered, deep in the hearts of many condemned and incarcerated people, the scattered traces of hope and humanity—seeds of restoration that come to astonishing life when nurtured by very simple interventions.

"Proximity has taught me some basic and humbling truths, including this vital lesson: each of us is more than the worst thing we've ever done."

THE EFFICIENT AMBASSADOR

The Ambassador is a 92-unit apartment building located at 37 Casco Street, which is pretty much where the Arts District, centered on Congress Street, meets West Bayside, just east of Cumberland Avenue. We bought it in 2016 as an eighty-six-unit apartment building and were able to find a number of under-utilized spaces to add another six units. Bianca, with whom I've worked for years, figured this out.

The original eighty-six apartments are all studios, each not quite 300 square feet. Every studio apartment has a central room running from the entry door to the exterior window, about twelve feet wide by twenty feet long. The room serves as bedroom, living room, study, and hobby center if you have a hobby or a craft. At the end, towards the apartment door just off the main room, is a kitchen, fully equipped and complete with appliances—about eight by four or five feet. The bathroom, about the same size, is on the other side of the kitchen. You access it by the bathroom door off the main room, towards the window at the exterior wall of the unit.

For those of you who have multiple possessions, tons of things, attics or basements full of stuff, or can't park your car in the garage due to all the stuff in it, these apartments should make you envious. Life in an Ambassador apartment is economic and efficient, the furthest thing from what is commonly referred to as a McMansion, or is, in affordable housing parlance, "over-housing."

To understand this latter term better, imagine a couple who live alone in a fairly large house, which in my neighborhood is at least 3,500 square feet, or over 1,700 square feet per person. Folks at the Ambassador live in 300 square feet, or about in eighteen percent of the space in which the West Ender does. That's efficient. And economical. Life simplified.

WAKE UP, OLD DOG

One evening over at some friends' house, I told the story of living in a major city in the 1980s at the age of nineteen, getting into a fight, and being thrown in jail. Gwendy, the daughter of our friends and a friend herself though over forty years younger than me, said, "Imagine if you were black." I felt my story of pain, poverty, and woe had been ignored, even belittled. I got up and left. Went home.

Gwendy's dad, who is a wonderful guy, came over to my house later that night to drink a beer with me and talk about something specific and about nothing. The following day, feeling uncertain about my behavior, maybe even a bit regretful, I went to the bookstore and bought Ta-Nehisi Coates' *Between the World and Me*, which dives deeply and personally into America's racial history. I read it intently and learned how much I didn't know about race. And that Gwendy had made a very good point that night.

I'm not aware of another place on earth so besmirched with this horrible white behavior.

AND NOTHING BUT THE TRUTH

In 2014, a fire in a rental building on Noyes Street killed six people unable to access the egresses. We did not own the building, nor did we know the landlord. This was a tragedy that didn't have to happen. Shortly after the fire, Portland created a housing safety office to keep tenants safe and landlords compliant with the code. The staff there are good people. We work well with them, as our interests are aligned: keeping people safe in their homes.

In order to pay for itself, the office requires landlords to register their units with information about the units by January 1—charging $35 (now $50) per apartment, which for us amounts to around $50,000. We pay every year.

We've it figured out now, but at the time when the office was newly formed, we and the city struggled to figure out exactly what to pay because there are a number of discounts one can apply to the cost, depending on certain life safety systems in the apartment building. Is it sprinkled ($10 off), does it have a monitored fire alarm system ($7.50 off), do you have a smoke-free policy ($2.50 off)? You could go from having to pay $35/unit to $15/unit, again a big difference for us, as we were managing and owning over 1,500 apartments in the city at the time.

In 2018 we saw that we'd not taken several discounts in 2017, and asked the housing safety office if we could have a few months to file while we worked to correct our registration rolls. They understood and allowed us the needed time. We got them our data within a month but had to rescind and redo just over 200 units where we realized we'd not filed for the appropriate discount. The HSO allowed us the time we needed without levying a late fine as the law permitted them.

In early March, the citywide newspaper printed a story entitled "Lack of Enforcement Leads to Fewer Portland Landlords Registering Rental Units." It named our company among a few others as the culprits. The reporter called me prior to writing the article, and I'd explained our situation and our solid and compliant relationship with the housing safety office. He used none of what I said. Instead, the article painted us in a bad light. Upon reading the article, I called the reporter and told him he had not told the detailed truth of the matter.

Is what you've read factual?

Yes.

Then the story is true.

No, it's not. It's like saying you got in a car accident and got injured without admitting that actually you were at fault and ran a red light and killed the other driver. It's half-truth, which is not the truth.

Is what I wrote factual?

The one fact out of ten I gave you? Yes, that one is true.

Then the story is true.

No, it's not. When you tell the truth, you tell the whole truth and nothing but the truth.

I was hung up on.

HOUSING, A RIGHT AND A PRIVILEGE

Housing is a right. It's every individual's right.

Maybe another way to say this is that everyone deserves housing, and we're a wealthy enough country that can find a way to afford it, if we're willing to work together, particularly the public officials and the private builders.

To suppose that housing is not a right would be inhumane and mean.

Housing is also a privilege, something we are fortunate to have if we have it and most of us do. Getting your license and driving the roads is often referred to as a privilege. And as best I can tell, privilege means "a right." But it's a special privilege, one that can be taken away from you if you don't follow the rules or abuse the rules, like driving while intoxicated, or driving to endanger.

The same is true of housing. You're granted the right to an apartment through an agreement, known as a lease, with the owner of the building. The lease outlines the responsibilities and obligations of the owner and of the tenant, those responsibilities and obligations that come with this privilege.

One obligation of the lessee, the tenant, is that he or she must pay rent, just as the owner of the building must pay the mortgage to the bank. A responsibility is that you, the tenant, respect the building, the apartment, and the other apartment dwellers, your neighbors.

When this obligation is broken, or you, the tenant, are found refusing common responsibilities, you may lose your privilege.

Housing is a right.

It's also a responsibility.

THAT GUY STOLE MY BIKE

Seems we should call things what they are. The late comedian George Carlin adamantly proposed this idea. He pondered, among other things, when did a jungle become a rain forest? A swamp a wetland? A store clerk a sales associate? An employee a team member?

In South Portland, the juvenile prison is called "the youth development center."

Folks who used to be called homeless, are now called people experiencing homelessness. The notion of experiencing implies to me that you are not accountable, that this current state of affairs was caused by others, that in no way was it your fault. Taking this a step further, we understand that you may have to eat, sleep, spend your day, pee and poo, and maybe pitch your tent wherever you feel you must, wherever you like that is otherwise a public place, like a park.

It became apparent last year when there were a number of public homeless encampments, that residents of Portland would no longer visit these parks, fearing erratic behaviors from the homeless population, many of whom were in the grips of substance use.

Hundreds of homeless people were encamped in what is called Harborview Park on West Commercial Street. For residents of the West End, traversing through this park presented the quickest way to get to Commercial Street, particularly by bike, since you would avoid the busy streets of State and High. That traversing stopped. Nobody went through the park. It'd been taken over by the homeless. It smelled of urine and feces. Used needles and orange needle caps littered the path and the sidewalk.

There were multiple bicycle chop shops in the encampments. I couldn't have been the only one to notice that many of the homeless rode very expensive bikes, some that were new that would go for upwards of $5,000. Beautiful bikes.

During the encampment year, my family had two bikes stolen from us; one from outside Portland High School, and one from our back porch. I saw the guy who stole the one from our house, except I only saw his upper torso and hat as he made his way out to the street. I was too late. I biked down to the Harborview encampment and told the cop parked in his patrol car in the lot abutting the park that the guy with the red sweatshirt and yellow hat had stolen my bike.

I pointed to the guy.

Cop: Is the bike there?

Tom: No.

Cop: If the bike isn't there, there's nothing I can do.

Tom: That sucks. Any idea what he might have done with my bike?

Cop: Took a picture of it, put it on Facebook Marketplace for a couple hundred bucks, sold it to some kid who's riding it around outside his house in his hometown.

Tom: But he'd need a cell phone to do that.

Cop: They all have cell phones.

SPINNING IN THEIR ORBITS

I understand that most of the homeless have had enormous trauma in their lives—ruinous, harmful trauma—most likely when they were children, most likely brought on by their parents or someone older in their extended family. And I understand there's an abundance of addiction. My guess is that for most of the homeless folks here in Portland things will likely remain the same for them: same addictions, same difficulties, same mental health issues.

Our city staff works diligently to find shelter for people, particularly as winter approaches. The local paper has written a number of stories on some of the homeless' refusal to go to the shelter. One man said he likes to have a beer in the evening, and this isn't allowed in the shelter. Another said they wouldn't let him take his dog with him. A third said that they separated the men from the women, and as a result he couldn't sleep with his girlfriend.

I understand. I have a drink before dinner. I sleep in the same bed with my wife, and our dog is one room over.

John Steinbeck's novel *Cannery Row* is a story about a small clan of homeless men who turn an old tin warehouse into a temporary home:

"Mack and the boys, too, spinning in their orbits. They are the virtues, the graces, the beauties of the hurried mangled craziness of Monterey and the cosmic Monterey where men in fear and hunger destroy their stomachs in the fight to secure food, where men hungering for love destroy everything lovable about them.

"Mack and the boys are the beauties, the virtues, the graces. In a world ruled by tigers with ulcers, rutted by strictured bulls, scavenged by blind jackals, Mack and the boys dine delicately with the tigers, fondle the frantic heifers, and wrap up the crumbs to feed the seagulls of cannery row. What can it profit a man to gain the whole world and come to his property with a gastric ulcer, a blown prostate, and bifocals?

"Mack and the boys avoid the trap, walk around the poison, step over the noose while a generation of trapped, poisoned, and trussed-up men scream at them and call them no-goods, come-to-bad-ends, blots-on-the-town, thieves, rascals, bums. Our father who art in nature, who has given the gift of survival to the coyote, the common brown rat, the English sparrow, the housefly and the moth, must have a great and overwhelming love for no-goods and blots-on-the-town and bums, and Mack and the boys. Virtues and graces and laziness and zest. Our father who art in nature."

I think for years the book gave me a false, romanticized version of the homeless, thinking them strong-willed, independent, non-conformist. Portland's homeless population is struggling, figuring out how to eat, where to sleep, how to survive. There is nothing romantic about it.

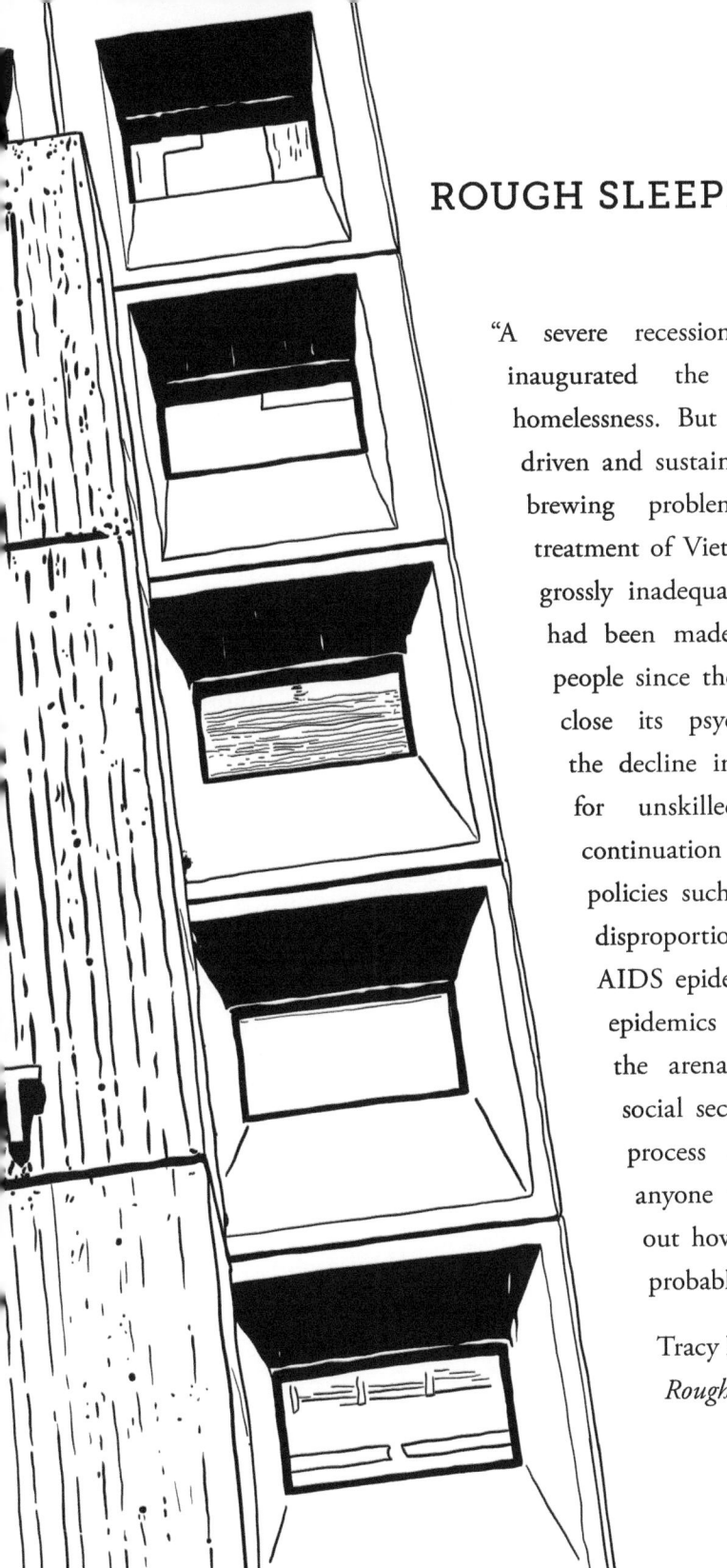

ROUGH SLEEPERS

"A severe recession in 1980 had inaugurated the era of rising homelessness. But the problem was driven and sustained by many long-brewing problems: the shabby treatment of Vietnam veterans, the grossly inadequate provisions that had been made for mentally ill people since the nation began to close its psychiatric hospitals; the decline in jobs and wages for unskilled workers; the continuation of racist housing policies such as redlining and disproportionate evictions, the AIDS epidemic and the drug epidemics that fed it. Also the arena of applying for social security disability—a process so complex that anyone who could figure out how to get assistance probably didn't need it."

Tracy Kidder
Rough Sleepers

THE ELECTRIC CHAIR

There are a number of low-income, affordable housing developments in my neighborhood, most closely across the street is the Butler School, and just behind that another on Carleton Street, both managed by the nonprofit Avesta Housing. Three blocks down at 284 Danforth stands a large brick L-shape building, maybe six-stories high, run by the Portland Housing Authority. Down the road on both sides of Danforth, running up to Spring Street, are hundreds of low-income housing apartments.

Many of the kids who lived there went to the nearby grammar school, Reiche, with my three kids. There are also group homes managed by full-time staff. The one I know of on my street, Pine Street, is mainly for younger folks, and one is just down Emery where a number of older folks reside. One of my neighbors across the street who lives at the Butler School, Frank, moves around using an electric wheelchair. He has the tiniest dog. The dog sits in his lap.

When the dog has to go, Frank puts him on a leash. The dog walks in front like he's pulling Frank in his chair. A little bit like Rudolph.

Another guy, John, who lives in a group home down Emery, was wheeling back from Cumberland Farms once and stopped dead in the middle of the Pine and Emery fork when his chair ran out of electricity.

> You run out of juice?
>
> Yes, I think so.
>
> Want me to push you?
>
> Please.

I'd been sitting on my porch.

I grabbed the back of the chair and pushed. It felt stuck in a low gear, making a whining chain-like noise. It was not in neutral.

I said nothing. Got pushing.

We were gaining momentum, me sort of running. Then suddenly, a hard stop.

I slammed into the back.

    What? What happened? What's the matter?

    Stop sign.

Sometime that past year, the city had installed a stop sign on Emery Street where it crosses Spruce. In my opinion (shared with my neighbors) no stop sign needed to be added, since a sign has always has been on Spruce Street, effectively keeping accidents from occurring. Having driven the road for thirty years with no stop sign and no need to stop, I forget about it. Not John, law-abiding chair driver.

I started pushing again. Got him up his ramp at his house, into his apartment.

ORDER

The odd thing about being a landlord—a good landlord with pride of ownership and stewardship—is that while, like so many other businesses you're delivering a good product (a refurbished apartment) and good service (maintenance 24/7) you're also constantly enforcing building rules, ironically for the benefit of the larger tenant community—the people who live there.

Some of the rules we enforce seem silly and can bother tenants. An obvious one being that we don't allow shoes to be placed in the hall outside the door. The tenant just wants to keep the apartment clean. The problem, as the landlord, is that if one tenant does this, all will follow and you will have a hall of shoes, a messy common area that, yes, tenants will be displeased with. Also, according to the fire department, shoes in the hallway are considered an "obstruction," so by Portland code, not allowed.

If you're having trouble with your neighbor for whatever reason—noise, smell of smoke, too many visitors, some seemingly dangerous or criminal activity—and you call the police, the police will tell you to call your landlord.

We get those calls.

THE POLICE!

The police: We're so glad you guys bought this building.

Muscle: Thanks. Why?

The police: It's a hotspot for us.

Muscle: What's a hotspot?

The police: A building where we get multiple 911 calls.

Muscle: How many times have you been called here?

The police: This year? Two hundred.

DISORDER

(a) No person shall occupy any dwelling...or rooming unit...which is a disorderly house as defined herein.

(b) A "disorderly house" is any building which:

1) the police have visited a minimum number of times in a 30-day period...In response to situations which are created by the owners, tenants, and guests and which would have a tendency to unreasonably disturb the community. The neighborhood or an ordinary individual in the vicinity...including but not limited to loud music, boisterous parties...loud noise or fights...tenants being intoxicated on public in the vicinity of the building...

2) the police have visited 3 or more times in 30 days in response to situations which...constitute either a crime or civil infraction... or create a reasonable suspicious that illegal drug use or sales or prostitution or public indecency...

From the City of Portland, Maine
Code of Ordinances, Disorderly House Ordinance
Buildings and Building Regulations, Chapter 6

A MESS TWO DOORS DOWN

133-135 Emery Street sits two doors down from where Judy and I live. It's a six-unit building in decent shape. The tenants that come and go seem nice. Just the opposite some years ago. From roughly 2012 to 2017, the landlord, an infamous slumlord later sued by the city for another building she owned, on grounds it was disorderly and riddled with code violations, did nothing to help us—her neighbors—by doing simple things like screening tenants or installing porch lighting.

In this particular building on Emery Street, there were multiple girlfriend-boyfriend fights outside, verbal and physical. They had fires in the backyard, burning anything available including tires: black fumes, horrible smells, loud voices in the middle of the night. The police had been there several times for all manner of things, mostly drug dealing and overdosing and domestic violence.

The Drug Enforcement Agency had been there multiple times too, once with a battering ram.

We live in a busy place and have all kinds of neighbors of all kinds of incomes, issues, ages, and ethnicities. We have three children. The kids learned firsthand what people strung-out on drugs look like and act like. They saw couples fight, sometimes physically, most always loud.

UNCONTROLLABLE

In our small city, with government-controlled pricing of apartments, it would imply that you, as the owner of an apartment building, could control the other side of the cash flow statement—the expenses.

You would think.

You'd be wrong.

There are certain expenses we call "uncontrollable," meaning you as the property owner have no say—no control—over their costs. Those items being real estate taxes, utility rates, insurance, fuel costs, and interest rates. The last one, interest rates, may seem boring, even benign, when it's really nothing but. It can upend you because interest rates change all the time, daily, weekly, monthly, year after year, and should they increase, you must pay the bank a higher monthly mortgage, which leaves you not enough money to maintain and manage apartment buildings.

It's a recipe for bankruptcy.

I wouldn't be alone in suggesting you not go into a business where you can't keep up with your expenses.

Portland apartment buildings have become too much of a risk for anyone to invest in them or improve them. And so that period of obsolescence that we so successfully beat back over the last thirty years, is creeping in again, uncontrollably.

LUNCH LOST

Commentator John: She had a whole week's worth of lunch and lost it!

Commentator Gail: She didn't lose it. We know exactly where it is, it's all over the third row.

From the movie, *Pitch Perfect*

When you're dizzy and nauseous every morning, you'd like to think you can purge the feeling with one good hurl. Not so. Just the opposite. The medical community calls it "habituation," where you're supposed to lean into your crappy feeling and do things that provoke your symptoms, in this case to make myself dizzy, such things as balancing on one foot with your eyes closed, or moving your head up and down and left and right, and repeat.

ETERNAL RECURRENCE

"All over all over again? As if.
 Not on your life, Watson, not in this life.
 This little bump in the road is that one
 That so jolted you, you figured
"I'm done."
 But the fires of Hell on earth keep grilling
 You, buddy, overdone yet still willing to take it, that nothing you've got left
 now like then, ashes
 of ashes, snow on snow."

"Eternal Recurrence," Michael Pettit, *Blue Angel*

BOY IN THE PLASTIC BUBBLE

As a kid growing up in Massachusetts in the mid 1970s, a TV movie came out called *The Boy in the Plastic Bubble*. The boy, a teenager played by a twenty-two-year-old John Travolta, is born with a deficient immune system, and so must live his life hermetically sealed-off from the rest of the world in the plastic bubble.

I woke up recently on a particular morning, frightened, anxious, and crying from a bad dream in which I was sobbing—apologizing to my dad and sister Jackie for being the boy in the plastic bubble.

My vertebral disorder is invisible. Pretty much every day I live with dizziness, lightheadedness, and nausea.

My private bubble.

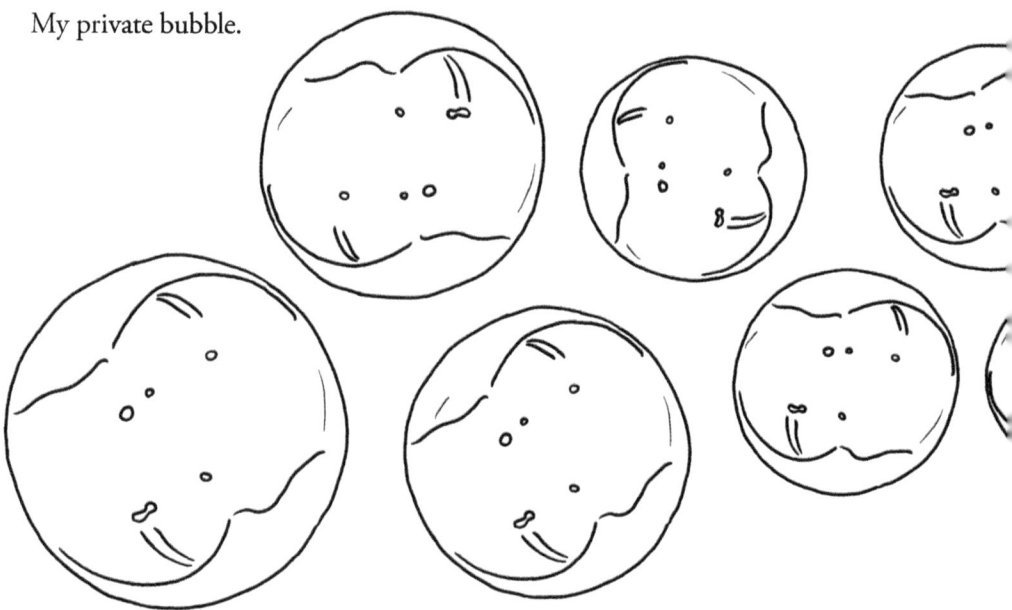

TANGENTIALITY (SQUIRREL!!)

Behavioral observations and mental status
Neuropsychological re-evaluation
January 9, 2024

Mr. Watson and his wife Judy arrived on time. He was casually dressed and well-groomed. Speech was normal in rate and rhythm. Thought process was typically linear and goal directed with occasional tangentiality. There was no evidence for thought disorganization. Mood was content and affective range was within normal limits. He reported coming to the appointment at the urging of his wife for re-evaluation.

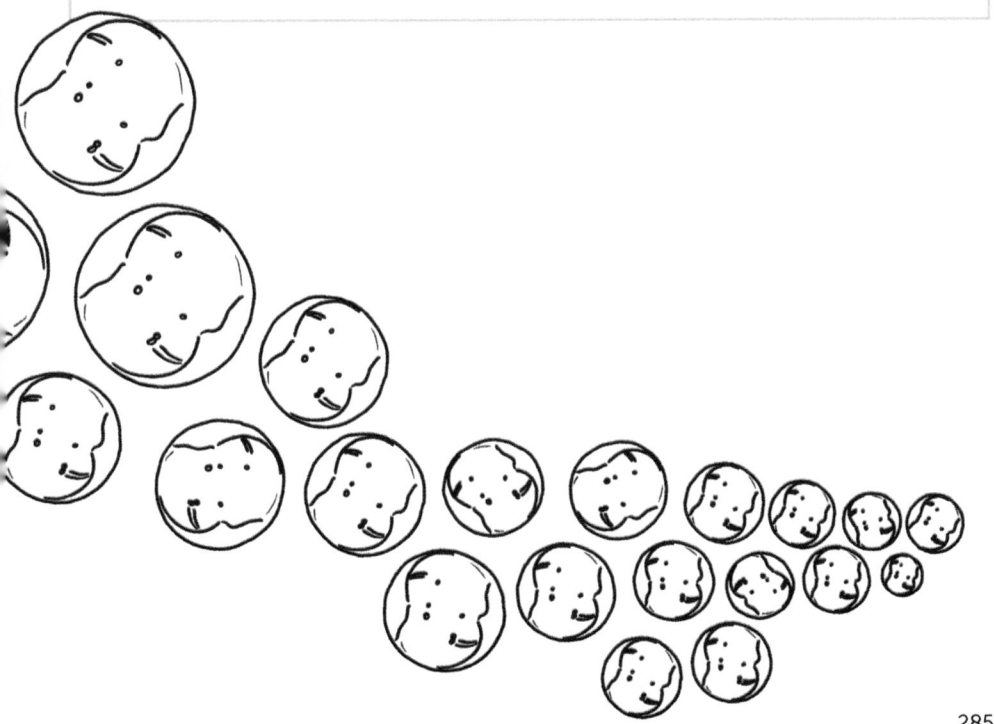

SKILLED INTERVENTION

New England Rehabilitation Hospital
Physical Therapy Documentation
September 23, 2024

High level balance acts are still very challenging

Skilled intervention required to challenge balance with eyes closed and hands on hip

Single leg stances were a challenge and could not hold position w/o touching side rails or moving out of position

Insight education: demonstrates awareness of current limitations and deficits

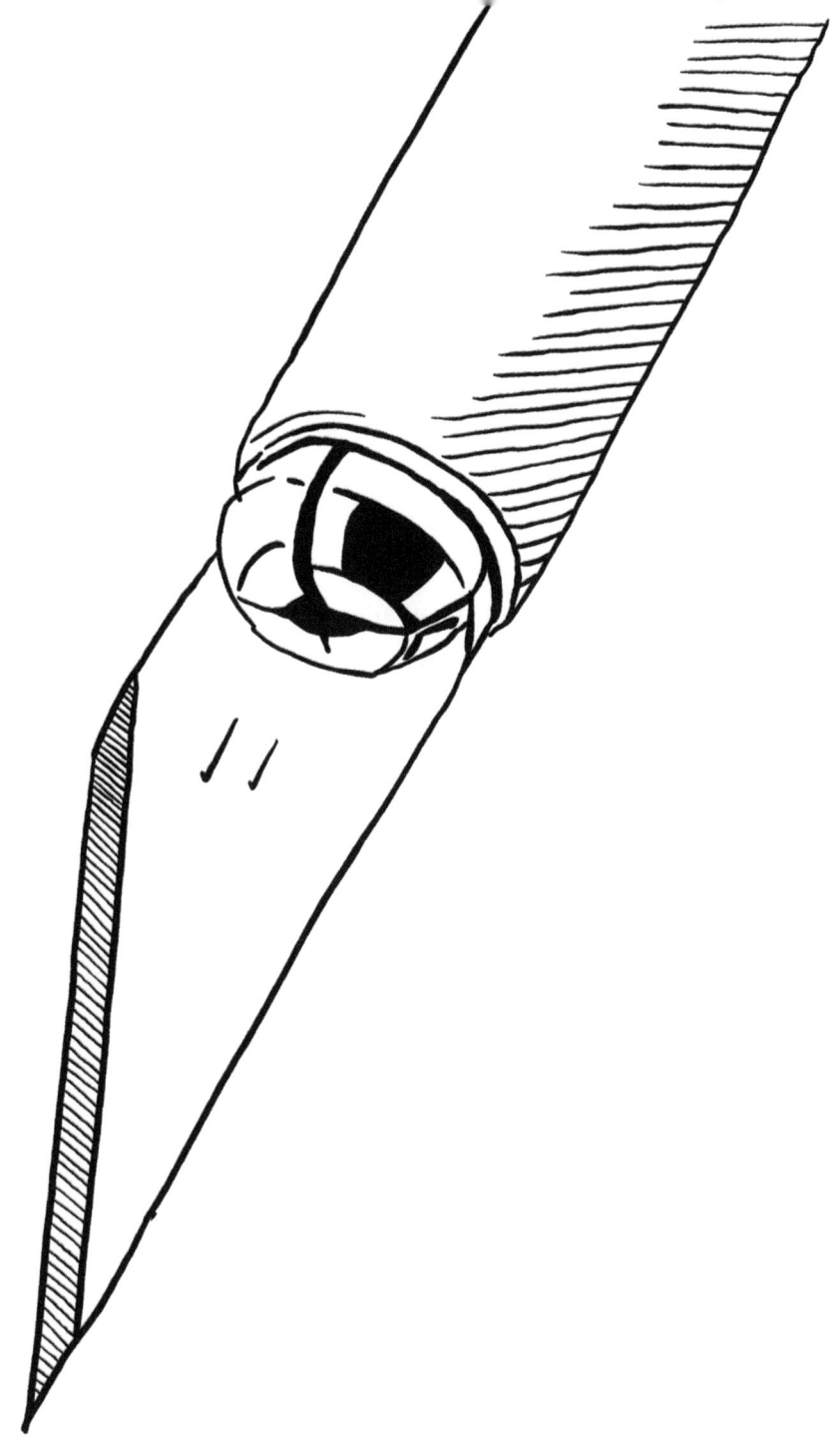

A SAFE PREDICTABLE ENVIRONMENT

New England Rehabilitation Hospital
Physical Therapy Documentation
May 14, 2024

Tom will perform habituation activities at home, but only in a safe, predictable environment with supervision.

He will walk, performing head turns and nods as he goes.

Walking forward, turn head to one side for about three strides, then either return to straight ahead orientation or turn head directly to the other side. Repeat.

Ideally someone else will call out the directions so it is not predictable, but if this is not practical, self-directed is ok.

Next complete this with vertical motions. Diagonals can also be introduced if any of this results in dizziness that persists.

PROVOKE THE PATIENT'S SYMPTOMS

"Habituation exercise is used to treat symptoms of dizziness… For patients who report increased dizziness when they move around, especially when they make quick head movements, or when they change positions like when they bend over or look up too much above their heads. Also, habituation exercise is appropriate for patients who report increased dizziness in visually stimulating environments, like shopping malls and grocery stores…

"The goal of habituation exercise is to reduce the dizziness through repeated exposure to specific movements… That provokes the patient's dizziness.

"These exercises are designed to mildly, or at most, moderately provoke the patient's symptoms of dizziness.

"Over time, with good compliance and perseverance, the dizziness intensity can reduce due to the brain learning to ignore the abnormal signal."

Vestibular.org

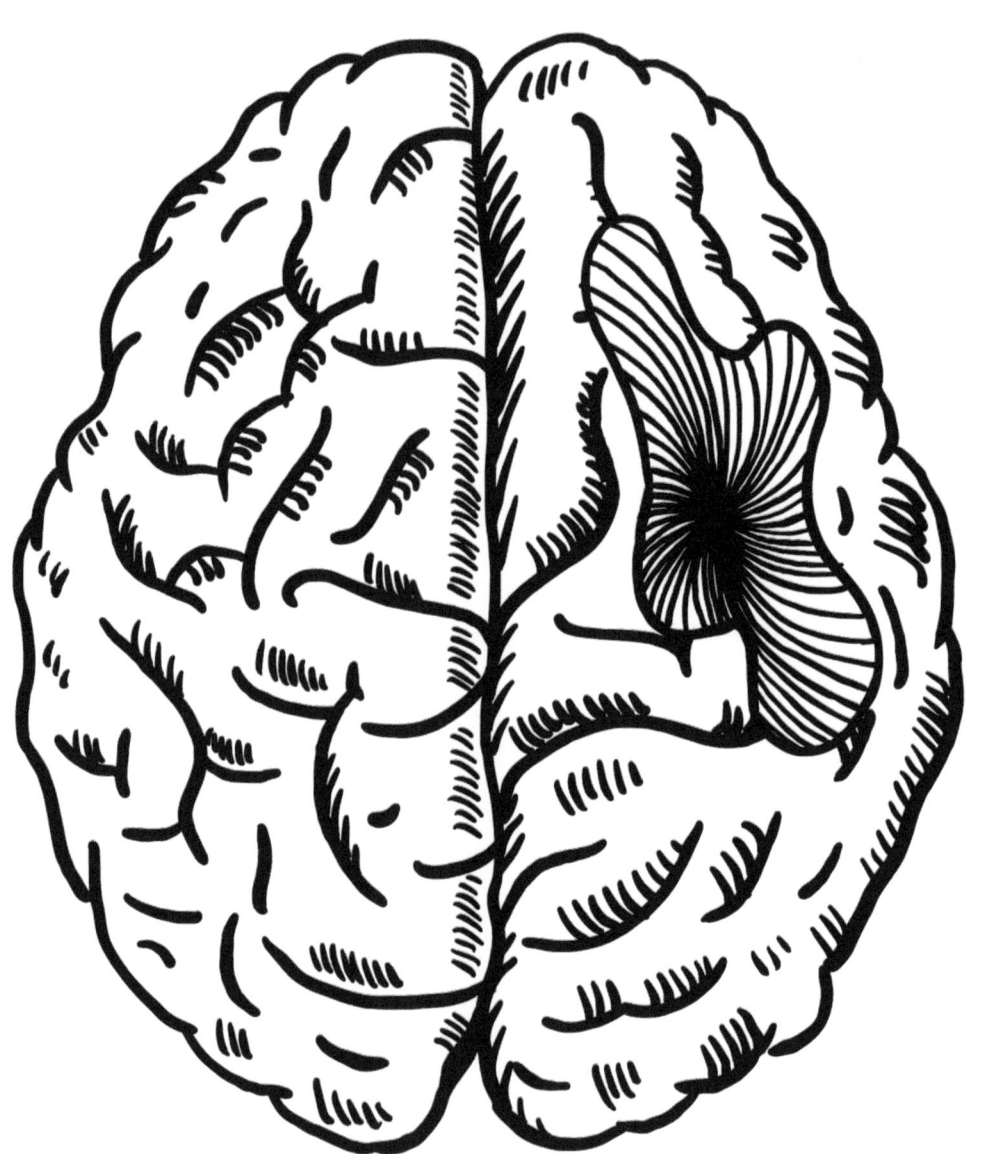

THE SPLOTCH

If you were to look at a picture of my brain, you'd see a number of small black dots and one large black dot among the gray matter. The smaller black dots are from strokes I've had over the last ten or twelve years. The large dot, more of a splotch, is the location of my equilibrium center, or what had been my equilibrium center. It took the brunt of the released blood clots.

OFF-BALANCE

"Good balance is often taken for granted. Most people don't find it difficult to walk across a gravel driveway, transition from walking on a sidewalk to grass, or get out of bed in the middle of the night without stumbling. However, with impaired balance, such activities can be extremely fatiguing and sometimes dangerous."

Vestibular.org

DAILY NAUSEA

Neuropsychological re-evaluation
January 9, 2024

He experiences daily nausea and dizziness but stated that it is not interfering a lot with his day... He holds onto the banister when using the stairs and takes the elevator instead of twisty stairs at work as it causes nausea, imbalance, and dizziness. His wife is managing the home finances at this time.

BARF BAG

The EMTs and everyone in the medical profession call them emesis bags. They're barf bags, used by folks who get motion sickness in the car or plane, and need to barf. Hospitals and EMTs carry them. The opening at the top is a plastic ring about four inches in diameter, and the bag that holds the vomit is just over four inches wide and the length of a quart bottle that can hold over a quart of vomit.

The bag is usually blue and translucent. There are gradations on the bag, starting at 4 ounces from the bottom, each gradient increasing by 4 ounces until it gets to 36 ounces, half a cup over a quart. This allows the medical professional holding the bag to know how much vomit the patient has vomited.

It's all I remember from the day of the stroke.

I awoke briefly, prostrate, while being wheeled on the gurney through the ER fast on the way to the OR. I threw up in the emesis bag after the ring was perfectly placed over my mouth. I let it fly. I remember thinking, briefly, what a great invention. The bag was invented by a guy from North Dakota named Gilmore Schjeldahl, an industrial designer known for his work with plastic bags. He created it for Northwest Orient Airlines.

Recently at physical therapy, I noticed a stack of these bags on the counter. "Oh wow, I've used one of those!"

In the spring of 2024, the makers of Dramamine (the motion sickness pill) opened an exhibit in which multiple barf bags were pinned to the wall by collectors.

The display's title: "The last barf bag."

BLOOD THIRSTY

"Physical activity is helpful not only because it creates new neurons but because the mind is based in the brain, and the brain needs oxygen. Walking, cycling, or cardiovascular exercise strengthens the heart and helps people who engage in these activities feel mentally sharper…

"Exercise stimulates your sensory and motor cortices and maintains your brain's balance system."

Norman Doidge, *The Brain That Changes Itself*

ALCOHOL BAD

Since the brain injury, I spend a fair amount of time and mental energy keeping nausea from getting in the way of my day. By early evening, I'm wiped out. Having alcohol, post-stroke, is probably one of the worst things a stroke-survivor, should be doing. But alcohol, a small amount, maybe six ounces of white wine, is ballast when it hits me. Or at least it feels that way.

Having spent the day, nauseous, sometimes wobbly, careful not to do anything quickly for fear of an onset of dizziness, the wine is a calming effect. It seems a stoppage of mental energy around my imbalance.

Growing up in the 70s, Lay's Potato Chips ran a nonstop effective brand campaign with the motto: "Betcha can't eat just one." That is true of Lay's and just about any other bag of chips I've opened. The problem with alcohol, in my case white wine, is that it's similar to the chips—hard to have just one. Often, I have a second. Actually, usually.

But then it has to stop.

If I have any more than the aforementioned two, I'm in trouble, most notably the next day. Not hungover. Not that. The dizziness, it really kicks in. I'm holding on to walls.

Mornings, regardless of the previous night's affairs, are difficult for me. For months I could not put my socks on, or my underwear, without a lot of patience. As far as the underwear is concerned, I could absolutely not do it standing up without falling into the bureau. I sat on the bed. Now it's over two and a half years, and I can now stand up and put my underwear on. Still, mornings are tricky.

Tricky because there is a lot of head movement putting on clothes, socks, shoes, leaning down to tie them, walking the dog who can't walk a straight line, bending over to pick up his poop, throwing it away, leaning over to put food in his bowl, grinding beans, heating and pouring water, cleaning dishes, turning to talk to Judy, turning to talk to our son, turning back to the toaster. Lots of multi-directional head movement. Some quick. It gets to me.

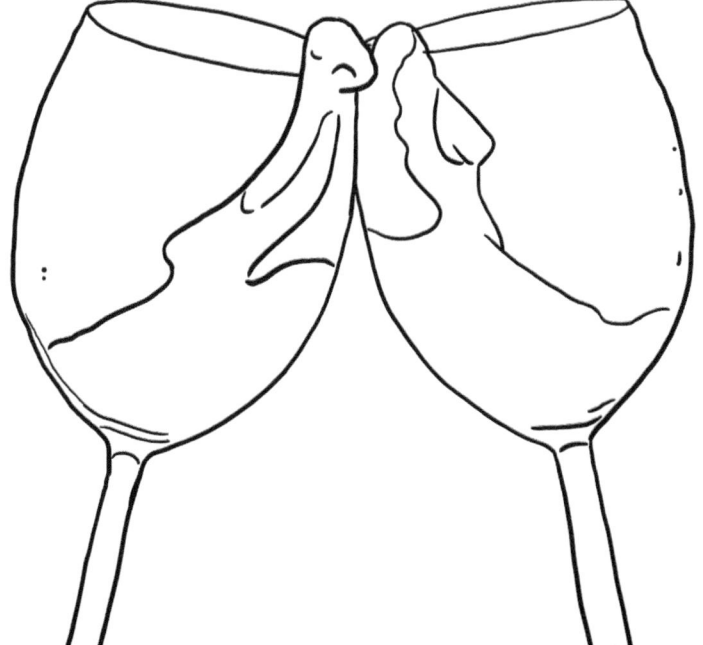

A SMALL PRICE

Bounce the ball.

Bounce the ball.

Pass it back and forth.

Walk, look straight up, straight down.

Again.

Again.

Walk, look left, look right, look left, look right, look left, look right.

I'M SORRY, WHO ARE YOU?

I've met all kinds of folks in the thirty-one years I've lived here: tradesmen, bankers, lawyers, lots of real estate people, ultimate frisbee teammates, co-workers, tenants, neighbors, and lots of fun, funny, nice folks that Judy has introduced me to. The last two years, post-stroke, I've struggled to put names to faces, something we all do, true; but, this go around it's been constant, a daily routine.

I know I know you. I just don't know who you are.

Not too long ago while on a run, coming right at me from the opposite direction, was a very happy familiar face.

>Tom!

>I'm sorry, who are you?

BALANCING ACT

New England Rehabilitation Hospital
Physical Therapy Documentation
September 23, 2024

Assessment

Patient impairments / limitations:

    Balance deficits

    Impaired activity & tolerance

    Impaired gait

Rehabilitation potential: good

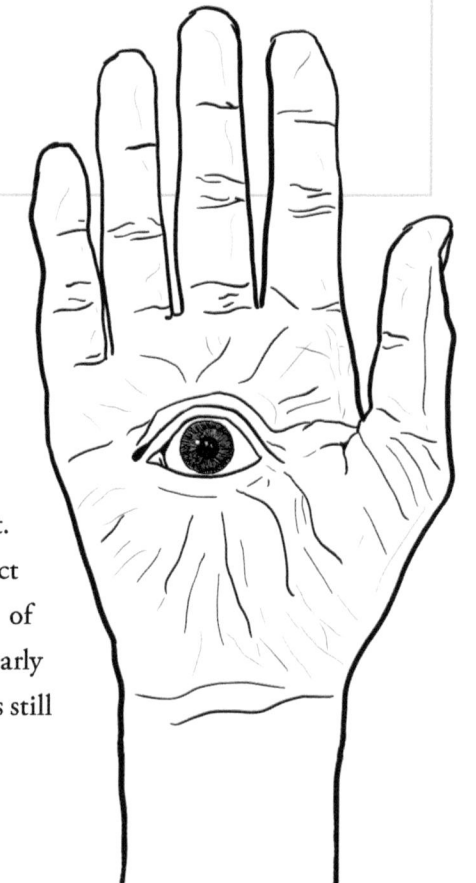

Recently, the physical therapists stopped throwing the ball with me. No more walking down the hall bouncing a ball. I played sports my whole life, baseball, basketball, and I can catch with either hand. Doesn't matter if it's a frisbee, a football, or a ping pong ball, I catch it. Apparently, the brain injury did not affect my hand-eye coordination. But the rest of my coordination, my balance even now nearly three years after the brain hit, the therapists still work on.

UNSTEADY

New England Rehabilitation Hospital
Physical therapy documentation
September 6, 2024

Tom presents today accompanied by his wife Judy for evaluation and treatment for report of dizziness, nausea, and imbalance.... Likens dizziness to feeling "off, like I have a head cold." Denies room spinning. Rates sensation on a scale of 1 to 5 currently at a 2.3: "Room spinning would definitely be a 5." Finds enjoyment in reading and writing. Expresses passion in his work as a real estate developer. Judy adds that when walking around in a circle, like when ascending or descending multiple flights of stairs, he experiences increased dizziness.

Tom states that he would like to return to prior level of function with regard to running and biking.

His wife contributes that when he is running or biking and looks over his shoulder, he experiences some unsteadiness.

BURST PIPE 2

The interior of an artery in my neck split, released clots into parts of my brain cutting off oxygen supply, and in doing so nearly killed me, and left me with a brain injury. I'd been a ticking time bomb, as the saying goes, and didn't know it.

What would keep this from happening again?

The slightest pain in my neck brought on this thought. It brought on depression. I found it hard to avoid the DWARVES: dread, worries, anxiety, regrets, victimhood, emptiness, and self-loathing.

What brought it on?

Did I drink too much?

Probably. And while not advisable, I had fun.

Work myself to death?

No. I like work.

Too much stress?

Too much?

No.

Stress?

Yes.

How does the inside of an artery split?

What had I done?

At some point I'd had enough of myself, of my crying, of my dwelling in depression, of my wallowing in victimhood, of my fears of recurrence. At some point it all felt solipsistic and self-absorbed. At some point I thought, okay, keep an eye on yourself, those dwarves are not to be ignored.

Observe myself instead of critique myself.

And try to learn about what I sensed and what I experienced.

It was bad enough feeling bad.

No need to feel bad about feeling bad.

I made a decision to get out of my head, to get out of the house and engage. Yes. Life was out there.

LIFE BEGINS

"Life begins at the end of your comfort zone."

Neale Donald Walsch

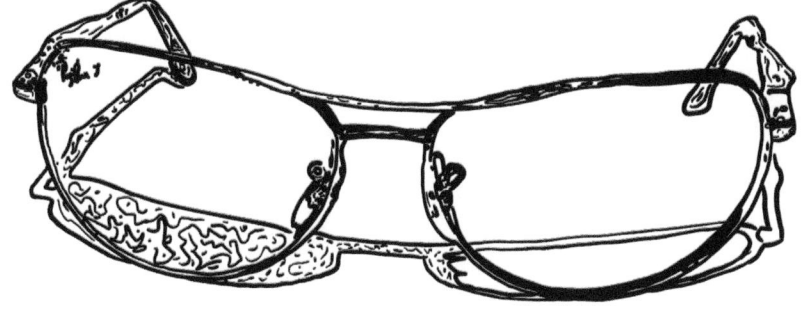

EASIER SAID THAN DONE

Depression is no fun and it's hard to get out of it. Usually, it entails a spiraling downward. You try to figure why you're depressed. Just doing that alone is depressing, since it rarely proves fruitful. Even if you can find a reason or two, you're still depressed. And you get depressed about being depressed.

It doesn't like to stop, this depression.

It gets worse.

It seems to consume you.

I tried to outrun it.

I ran. And kept running. Sometime double-digit miles.

This seemed to chase the darkness away, a kind of physical respite.

Inevitably, for me, it re-surfaced.

My whole life.

After the stroke, depression and anxiety roared into my head and body. I cried every day. That's when the neurologists insisted that I meditate and/or medicate. I've been doing both now for two years and while I still have some depression and anxiety, I have no more long dark periods and no more panic attacks in the middle of the night.

I'm thankful for these less frequent and shorter episodes of darkness. Instead of trying to understand the reasons, which I found over the years often worsened my condition, I now observe myself and I observe the mental pain and anguish, and this sort of removing myself from myself has helped extinguish it from time to time.

I observe it. I see it. It's part of me.

This is not easy to do. Nor easy to accept. It's work.

I have to stop the reeling. Remind myself to watch and observe.

Way easier said than done.

DEPRESSION: 3 POSITIVES

Ironically, there are positive benefits to depression, namely: 1) uncertainty, 2) empathy, and 3) strength.

I think uncertainty is beneficial. It's good for us. It's like a gift if we take advantage of it. When we're uncertain about a person, situation, problem, or potential opportunity, we think on it. We explore options and possibilities. We consider alternatives and outcomes. When we are uncertain, we're sometimes doing our best thinking.

Depression has from time to time left me uncertain. And so, I explore options I would not have otherwise. Things were unclear and there's a power in that, the power of hope and possibility and of something different coming (and over decades, the power of action and expectation and change). This is not to say to wallow, but rather to see that indeed you are uncertain and have much to explore out there.

How lucky are we to be uncertain. Don't take your luck lightly.

Sometimes depression scares me.

It gets in the way of me just living my life. Sometimes it's hard to get out of bed. So now I know why some people have trouble getting out of bed. That's empathy. If you've been down in the dumps and had some rough days, you begin to understand how it is with others.

Empathy and understanding are two traits, among others, that make great leaders. Or in most of our cases, empathy and understanding make us good people.

There's an old adage in sports: "No pain, no gain." The notion of incurring physical pain through training is likely dated, given how measured and gradual and smart and less punishing athletic training has become. Still, working through pain—mental, physical—makes you stronger.

Depression—that internal sinking feeling like you're drowning, feeling your head in a fog, the picking on yourself, the sometimes-concurrent anxiety, the inability to see things, trees, plants, the difficulty in relating to others, the inability to be happy for someone…. It's hell, it's painful.

Dealing with darkness, while maybe enervating, makes you stronger. People who have depression and are working through it, are some of the strongest people I know. These bouts are difficult times. You're working your way through what many folks won't acknowledge: mental difficulty. You are often on your own.

But keep going. Get help from others. Help is good. It saved my life.

LIGHTNESS & DARKNESS: 4 POSITIVES

In 1989, two women, Amy Ray and Emily Saliers, also known as the Indigo Girls, put out a song, "Closer to Fine," that became a huge hit. The song, as I understand it, is their eschewing commonly known methods of self-knowledge and self-awareness. Meaning, things like academic study or even drinking in a bar. The return in that song speaks to this: "The less I seek my source, the closer I am to fine."

While this line is probably the most quoted and most memorable, there's another one that speaks to depression, one of the main threads of the song: "Darkness has a hunger that's insatiable; lightness has a call that's hard to hear."

The darkness referenced is depression, something that seems to come over you, that you try to understand (Why do I feel this way?) or try to figure out (Is it because of this bad situation I'm in, difficulties at home as a kid? Should I see a therapist? Should I seek religion? What should I do next?). Why? Why? Why?

In 1989, at age twenty-six, I found myself depressed and seeking why, unsuccessfully. To make matters worse, as I did for years—probably close to fifty years—was pile on anxiety and self-loathing for being depressed, making my depression worse. My anxiety and depression, which I believe I had since I was twelve, made life difficult.

Getting out of bed could be an accomplishment. Trying not to show my mood—hiding my feelings could be hard. But I did it. Never showed.

It was killing me. It arguably was the reason I had a stroke.

I worked hard. Played sports hard.

Drank hard. All to avoid the darkness.

These did not work. I had a stroke. I'm lucky to be alive.

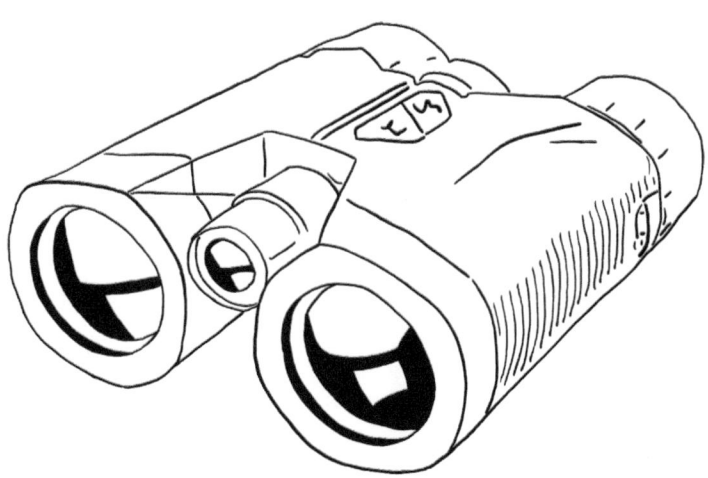

LIGHTNESS & DARKNESS: 4 POSITIVES CONTINUED

I did four things.

1. Medicate—the therapist told me three things:
    a. You are not a failure taking these meds.
    b. Many people take them and they have changed people's lives.
    c. Less time on anxiety and depression, means other worthy pursuits and thoughts.

2. Meditate—the neurologist told me to get an app.
    a. I got an app. It became a springboard.
    b. I meditate for an hour every day.

3. Read—Thich Nhat Hahn's works teach among other things:
    a. Have good thoughts.
    b. Use good words.
    c. Do good things.

4. Run—Wipes away stress. Clears the head.

DWARVES

D—dread
W—worries
A—anxieties
R—regrets
V—victimhood
E—emptiness
S—self-loathing

There seems no plausible way to eradicate the dwarves.

More often than not the reasons are unclear and maybe unknowable; and these sensations, feelings, call them what you will, surface randomly. They occupy the mind, manifest in the body: tight shoulders, a headache, nausea, tiredness.

The best I've found I can do is to follow Muscle's advice on this and "change the channel." Initially I thought this to be avoidance or suppression, and it may be, but dwelling and thinking intensely doesn't seem to solve the problem, or make it go away and can often make it worse or last longer. We sit and watch a horrible movie on maybe a slightly fuzzy screen—what do we do? We change the channel. Go for a walk. Go for a run.

> Put down the cell phone. Stop scrolling.
> Have coffee with a friend.
> Be kind. Help someone. Volunteer.

As hard as this may be, and it's hard when you're in the middle of what seems like hell, do these three things, if you can, throughout the day:

> Have good thoughts.
> Use good words.
> Do good things.

To the extent you can, make your struggles healthy ones.

HARDSHIP

"Your struggles develop your strength. When you go through hardship and decide not to surrender, that is strength."

A. Schwarzenegger

LIFE IS OUT THERE

When any one of the six dwarves takes hold, we tend to languish in it, we think on it, we feel, we wonder, we try to understand, we don't get it, or we don't like what we might have figured out, we have a rough morning, a rough day. There is this going inward.

I don't think this is a bad thing. I think sometimes it is best to lean into your pain. Give yourself some time with the hurt. When, however, we get negative, we'll pick on ourselves. We'll be depressed about being depressed, stressed about being stressed, and commonly anxiety begets more anxiety.

Stop.

Enough.

No more being hard on ourselves.

Life is doing enough of that to us.

Best to stop fighting yourself.

Suffering is not worth suffering for, as the Dalai Lama has said.

Begin instead to observe yourself. As best you can.

Not easy. Sometimes impossible.

Consider getting help. There are professional people you can talk to. That's what they get paid for. Many of them are very good at what they do, which is to help you.

Life is worth it. You are worth it.

To find life moves from going inward to outward.

Life is out there.

STAY ALIVE

In Matt Haig's wonderful memoir, *Reasons to Stay Alive*, he talks about his very dark and difficult bouts with depression, anxiety, and panic attacks. If you've experienced any of this, you may find parts of the book perhaps a bit frightening but ultimately resonant and helpful. Haig writes in the chapter entitled "running" that "running is a commonly cited alleviator of depression and anxiety." It certainly worked for me.

Prior to the brain injury I ran pretty much every day, miles commonly in the double digits: ten, eleven, twelve. Thirteen if I was really cruising. I'd run a couple marathons. But for a solid year and a half after the stroke, I did not run, until Judy got me to run our walks from one tree to the next.

Seems with each step my brain jiggles and I'm sure it doesn't, it just seems to have a direct line to where the feet meet the street feeling the impact. It's not much of an exaggeration to say there's a pounding in my head at each step. I told a friend that most folks feeling these symptoms of fogginess and nausea would wonder what was wrong with themselves and stop. I know what's wrong with me. I keep going.

Haig continues, "many of the physical symptoms of panic—the racing heart, the problematic breathing, the sweating—are experienced when running. So, as I began running again, I stopped worrying about my racing heart, because it had a reason to be racing. Also, it gave me something to think about. I was never the fittest person in the world, so running was quite difficult. It hurt. But that effort and discomfort was a great focuser. And so, I convinced myself that through training my body I was also training my mind. It was a kind of active meditation."

The nausea. The pounding. The fog. My brain injury. I seem to feel and hear every footstep, jarring my brain. I get lightheaded within a mile of starting. The wonderful physical therapists at New England Rehabilitation Hospital told me that I needed: "Repeated exposure to specific movements that provoke dizziness." Also known as habituation.

The more exposure, the more I get used to it and learn to manage it.

Running is quintessentially habituation. I run. I'm up to six miles.

SLOW AS SNAKE SHIT

These days I run slow, real slow. Looks like a glorified walk.

My friend Tim who drives a pickup, told me he struggled not to run me over and put me out my misery.

Thirteen-minute miles.

For those of you who run, you know how slow that is. It's slow.

It doesn't matter to me. It's meditation. It's time away.

Even with a brain injury it feels good to be out there, windy, snowing, raining. As long as I dress accordingly, I'm good.

My running Bible is Haruki Murakami's autobiographical view of running called *What I Talk About When I Talk About Running*. My good friend Malcolm, who also runs, bought me the book.

Murakami writes: "I don't care about the time I run. I can try all I want, but I doubt I'll ever be able to run the way I used to. I'm ready to accept that. It's not one of your happier realities, but that's what happens when you get older."

BECOMING HUNGRY

Having died and come back is one of the best things that's happened to me.

What exactly happened to me, physiologically, I'm not sure.

But spiritually—and, by this I mean my will, gut, heart—I left the hospital and became hungry for what was next in life.

I feel grateful and humbled.

I love my wife. She makes me laugh.

I love my family.

I have great kids: Rose, Audrey, and Sam. They make me laugh.

I have amazing friends.

The people I've met through work are smart and funny and good to be with.

I love my dog. He can't read. He makes me laugh.

DON'T BELIEVE YOUR OWN BULLSHIT

At some point, maybe the year after my brain injury, when my improvement seemed to plateau and stagnate, I found it easy to create a self-narrative of woe and victimhood. Interestingly, this thinking and feeling aggravated the dizziness and nausea. Like a lot of people, I can be emotional, and in this case, I was dwelling on my impaired physiology. I noticed this sort of a sustained negativism physically made me feel crappy.

At some point I had to stop this conflating of physiology with psychology. I found this unhealthy, this "woe-is-me" narrative. When people asked me how I was doing, I had reverted to that narrative: "I'm not sure," "Rough day," "This is hard," "I need to go home."

But I realized I could just as easily have said, "Good," "Beautiful day," "This is fun," "Let's do it again tomorrow."

As for that woeful self-narrative, I stopped.

I've told myself more than once: "Don't believe your own bullshit."

COGNITION OVERLOAD

My brain injury has some pretty obvious, or at least understandable, symptoms. A less noticeable but equally relatively constant is cognitive overload. You can sort of see my eyes gloss over. It's a state of mental exhaustion, where I don't have the ability or the capacity to take in any more information. I have to regroup.

What went on inside my brain, a lack of oxygen somewhere due to a blockage, maybe, is anybody's guess. There's no test or x-ray or picture that shows my processing and decision-making abilities having less capacity upon overuse. Nothing.

Luckily, I work with some really smart people who can calculate and dissect issues faster than most humans I know. Namely John and Joe who are both a decade or so younger than me. Since the brain injury, in order to keep up with them, I have to ask them to explain or re-state more often than I used to.

They're good with me, slowing down a bit to get me on track with them.

In any event, I tire. My brain gets exhausted.

To be certain, it's a good exhaustion.

Earned in good company.

DON'T CONFUSE YOUR FEELINGS WITH REALITY

I had a bad dream not long ago about being dizzy and unable to walk.

I woke up, crying. Sad and depressed.

I could lean into that emotion and think of how difficult life can be. I decided not to.

My emotions are part of me, but they are only part.

They get a seat at the table.

It's a big table.

There are a lot of seats.

IMPULSIVE

Neuropsychological re-evaluation
January 9, 2024

Impulsivity was noted on several occasions when he started tasks prior to the completion of instructions.

DOING EXTREMELY WELL

> Notes from visitation with Dr. P.
> September 26, 2024
>
> "He is almost three years out from his vertebral artery dissection and posterior circulation ischemic stroke. He seems to be doing extremely well…"

HAPPINESS

"Happiness can be found, even in the darkest of times,

If one only remembers to turn on the light."

Albus Dumbledore in J. K. Rowling,
Harry Potter and the Prisoner of Azkaban

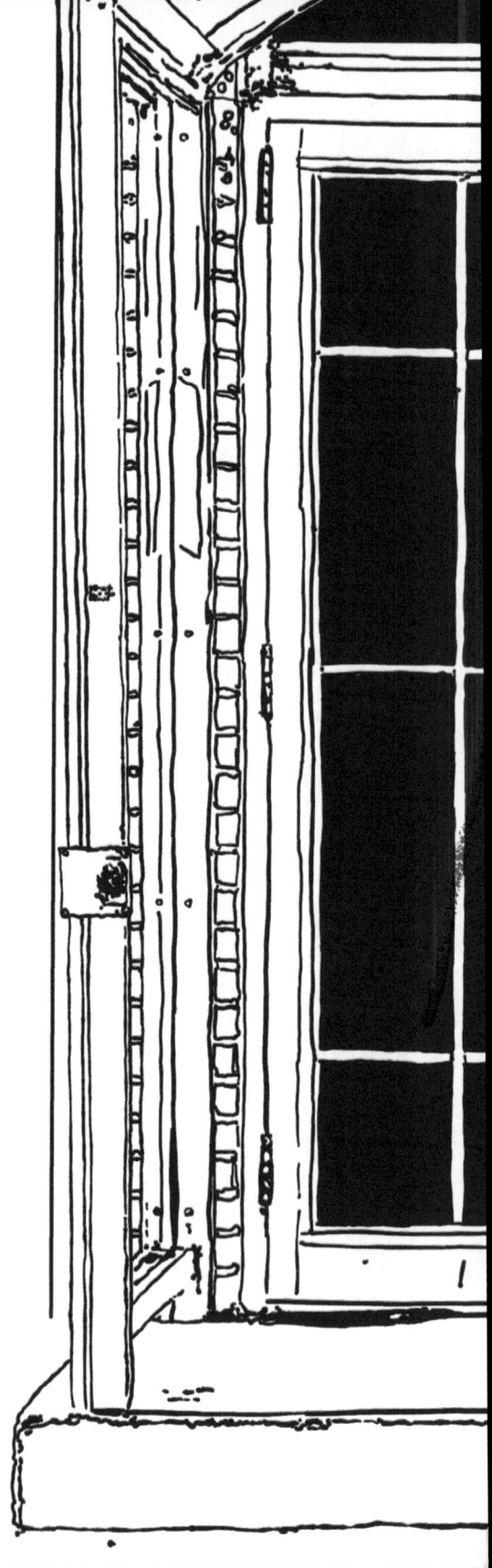

NOBODY MOVE

It's the classic bank robber line: You move, you may get shot.

That would hurt.

But we move. We have to move. It's part of our DNA. We walk, we run, we climb stairs, ride bikes, lift weights. We're much healthier—physically and mentally—when we work out or walk or play.

And, of course, in movement there's always the possibility of falling or getting hurt. We step into a hole while running, collide with a friend, jump and land awkwardly.

Still, some of the best of life is all about movement.

You may find when you move that you are at risk of falling.

A risk worth taking.

Every time.

AT RISK FOR FALLS

New England Rehabilitation Hospital
Physical therapy documentation
May 14, 2024

Assessment

Name of problem: Ability to climb stairs

Name of problem: At risk for falls

Name of problem: Bilateral hand weakness

Name of problem: Cognitive communication impairment

Name of problem: Dysarthria

Name of problem: Endurance

Name of problem: Executive function impairment

Name of problem: Gait difficulty

Name of problem: Fine motor coordination

Name of problem: Memory impairment

WORRIES

Neuropsychological re-evaluation
January 9, 2024

Mr. Watson's mood is more stable, and he feels more confident. He has more patience. He denies anxiety or panic attacks, but he worries about things.

MEMORY

Neuropsychological re-evaluation
January 9, 2024

From a cognitive standpoint, Mr. Watson is following group conversations better. He may have some difficulty persisting to task in situations in which he is fatigued or not fully interested. He continues to experience some difficulty with prospective memory when he has to remember to do something later in the day. His wife picks up on things and provides reminders and support to him. He may forget to write things down that he wants to remember. He takes time to think things through now. He uses his phone calendar inconsistently.

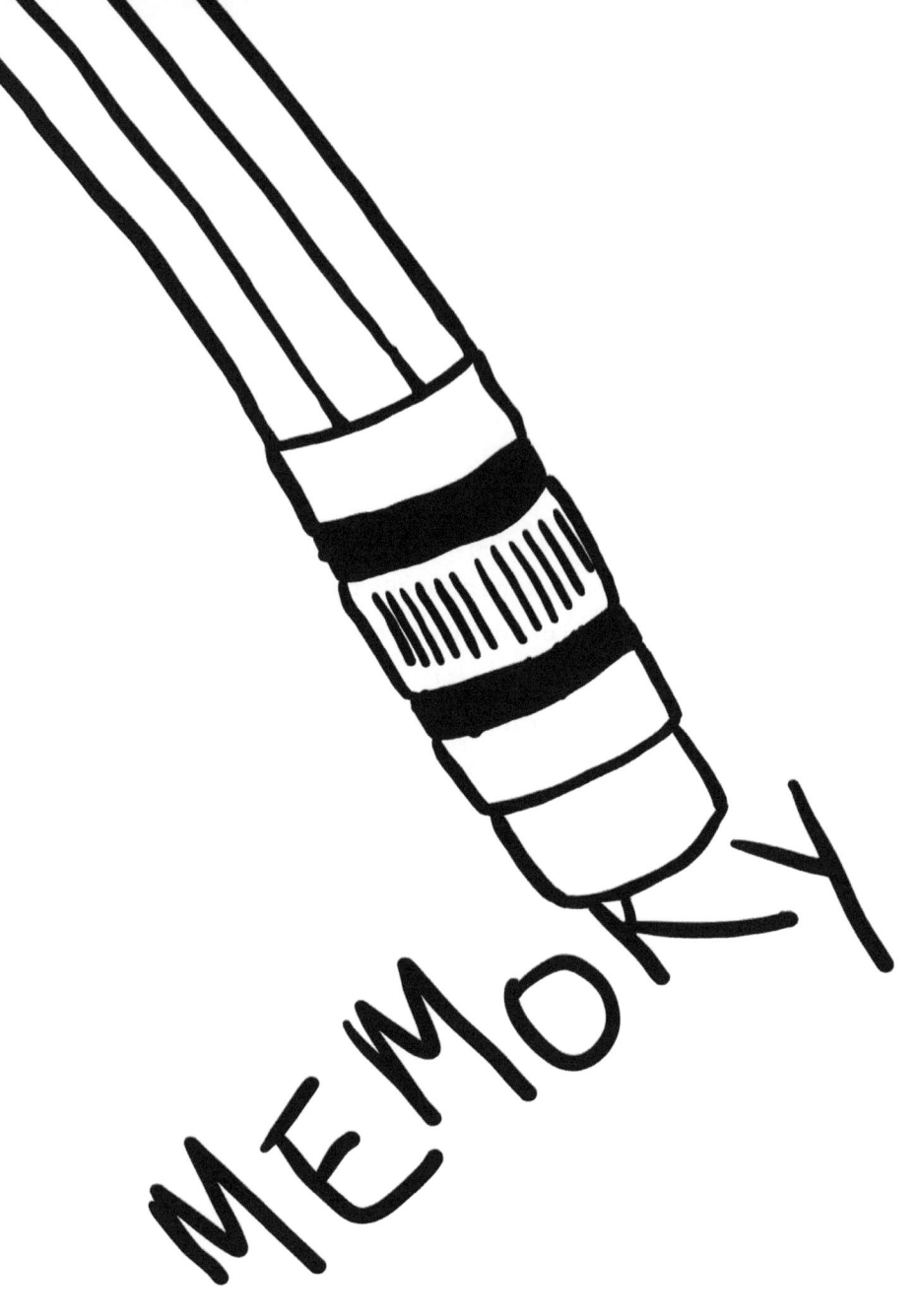

ON LIFE

"Nobody gets out alive."

Captain Jack (ninety-three years old)

THE BRILLIANCE OF STUPIDITY

After my brain injury, Judy told the neuropsychologist, "Tom is a high-level thinker," and that she wanted to make sure I regained that capacity. She said my friend Peter and I were the only two people she knew who thought at that level.

I'm not sure what that means.

I know I have to take out the garbage every Tuesday night.

Empty the poop-bag bucket.

Bring out the compost.

The recycling.

My colleague John and I sometimes look at each other after meetings—look at each other with laughable doubt, both of us uncertain what we should do next. The uncertainty might look like defeat, or bafflement, or even stupidity, but we've found by laying ourselves bare to a problem, being open to suggestion, even being vulnerable, meaning being open to options, leads us to re-thinking and in that, to new possible outcomes.

My friend Peter, who has multiple academic achievements, and who's since created and founded a pharmaceutical company and is now CEO of another, said to me after I told him I'd lost whatever money I had in a recent real estate deal, "Business is humbling."

He's a scientist and a businessman who understands the benefits of uncertainty, which leads to critical review and re-thinking.

In his book *Think Again*, Adam Grant extols the powerfulness of being uncertain: "If you're a scientist by trade, re-thinking is fundamental to your profession. You're paid to be constantly aware of the limits of your understanding. You're expected to doubt what you know, be curious about what you don't know and update your views based on new data…"

For John and Peter and me, "stupidity" is our term, just ours—nothing we share with anyone— to describe our uncertainty and the corresponding humility, knowing it is leading to new outcomes.

THE STUPIDITY OF BRILLIANCE

In 1991, John W. Gardner, in his commencement speech to the 100th graduating class at Stanford University said: "If I may offer you a simple mission: 'Be interested.' Everyone wants to be interest-ing, but the vitalizing thing is to be interest-ed. Keep your curiosity, your sense of wonder. Discover new things: care, take risk, reach out."

Too often, or more often than not, particularly in the world of business, "brilliance" is a pose, usually used by someone trying to explain how complicated things are.

They're not.

Brilliance tends to beget bloviation and over-complication.

What looks like brilliance is often just plain stupid, and definitely posing.

I'd suggest you not pose.

Rather, be interested. Take action. Take risk.

That's brilliance.

WHATEVER YOU DO, DON'T BE YOURSELF

This is not to say be phony.

No, it's more "Fake it till you make it," the well-known Alcoholics Anonymous adage.

I've now been doing what I do for over thirty years.

I've found most professionals don't want to work with someone who knows nothing, so I faked it by asking questions like, "Could you explain that? Maybe a little more in-depth?"

Imposter syndrome, as best I can tell, is feeling that you're not up to the task or not familiar with the task, so you feel somewhat inadequate.

People with big egos—almost always guys—decide to act like they know what they're talking about when they don't. And they keep talking. This is someone who believes his own bullshit.

If you're feeling imposter syndrome, I'd argue that's a good thing because it means you put yourself in an unfamiliar situation.

You have to listen. You have to watch. You have to think. You have to be ready.

Yeah, you don't know what you're doing.

Neither did anybody else when they started. It's okay not to know.

But don't avoid the situation, rather, fake it till you make it.

That's not to say you should bullshit someone.

Don't do that.

Do this:

    Be genuinely interested
    Ask good questions
    Use your resources
    Don't say what you don't know
    Listen
    Watch
    Think
    Be uncertain

INCREASED INVOLVEMENT

Neuropsychological re-evaluation
January 9, 2024

Mr. Watson has improved over the last year and a half and is working more now. He reported increased involvement in his real estate business. He has seventy-to-eighty employees working in his company and is involved in business meetings and decision-making.

2+2=4

IT'S TIME

At some point in your professional life, and for that matter your personal life too, you begin to realize that most of your life is behind you and far less is in front of you. This is when it may be best to take stock and come to understand that maybe it's time to step aside, perhaps gradually, but ultimately completely, and let the younger folks take their turn.

They're ready.

OBLIGATED

Recently at a CEO breakfast forum entitled "60 Ideas in 60 Minutes" where I sat as one of six panelists, I said there was no better time than now to try to cure your mental health issues, no matter how mild or strong, or no matter what your business or your business title.

I explained that my brain injury and augmentation of my depression and anxiety moved me to meditation and medication and the combination was saving my life. I implored the audience that should any of them be having difficulty grappling with mental health issues, they should seek help now.

Get to work on it, was my message.

Many people came up to me afterwards and thanked me, saying no one in business talks about mental health, and that we need to.

We have all kinds of physical ailments—intestinal, cancerous, cardio, pulmonary—all serious. Mental health issues are just that, ailments; and there are cures, or at least ways to improve. In the business world, a world in which I spend a lot of my day, it is time to talk openly about our mental health.

This is not an edict for you to wallow in your pain, or to "overshare," or make excuses for absenteeism, tardiness, or poor performance. Just the opposite.

You're obligated to improve yourself—for yourself and for others—and get better so you can live life fully, feel gratitude, help others, jump when jumping is called for, and to laugh and have fun. Indulge yourself. Oblige yourself.

YOU WILL DO GREAT

I still struggle to tie my shoes. I've lost speed typing and hit the caps lock button frequently. I slur certain words. I'm nauseous just about every morning. I'm on certain meds. Plus, a blood thinner.

I worry about a recurrence, not a lot, but sometimes.

Mostly I'm excited about today and tomorrow.

I'm very aware of my impermanence. That a lot of my life is behind me, not in front of me. That's if you're counting by years. Which I'm not.

I feel like the best is ahead of me.

Probably the single most gratifying feeling that's come over me in this post traumatic growth period is that, as they say, I've had a good run.

And now, as they also say, it's your turn.

You will do great.

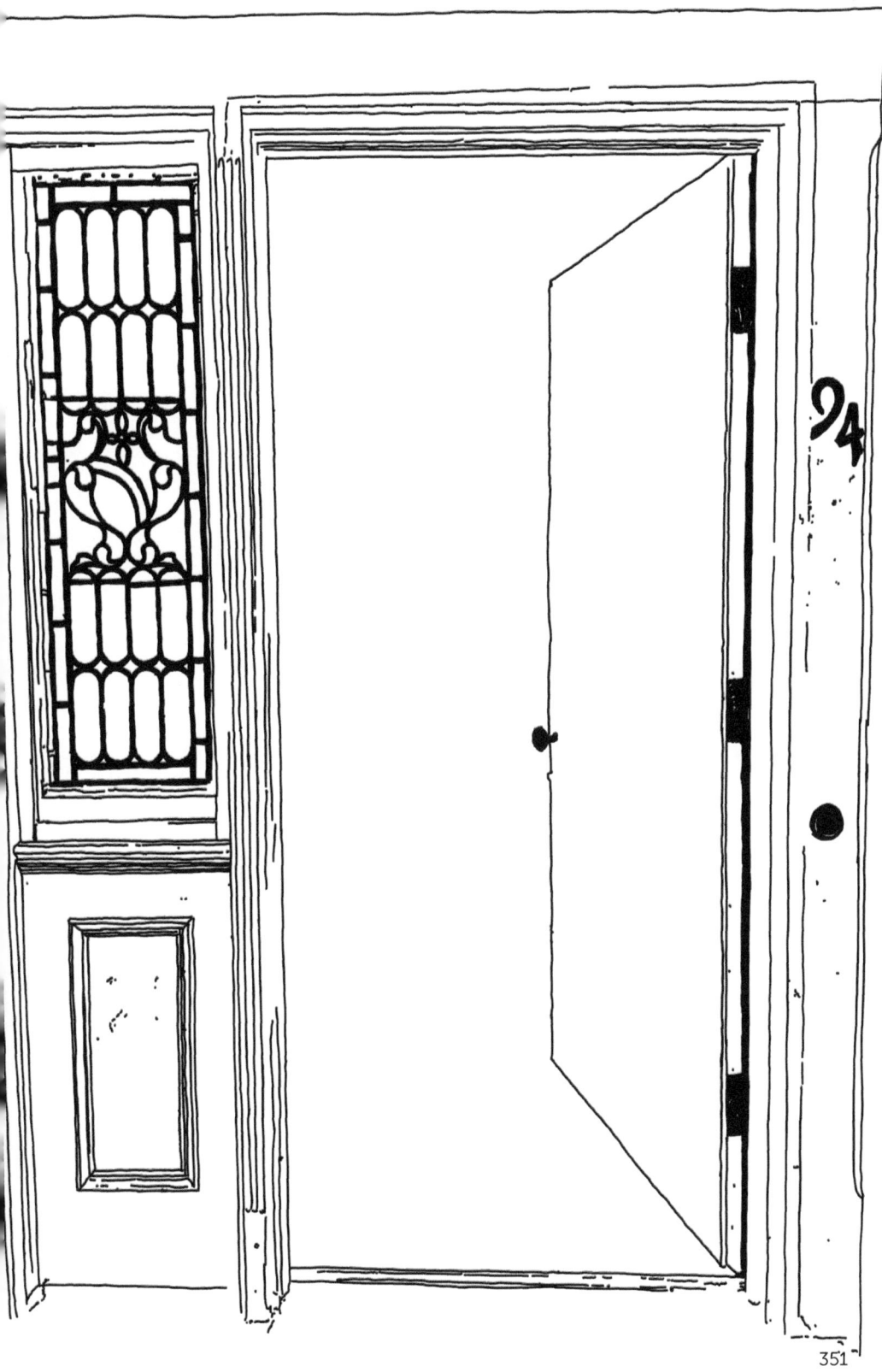

ACKNOWLEDGMENTS

I've come to realize that all of us are many things: husband, dog-walker, mother, father, wife, lover, thinker, worker, runner, son, daughter. Multitudinous as we may be, very few of us can claim we came by these roles and traits independently. Nor would we want to. Many people in our lives have played a part in shaping us, just as we have played a part in shaping them. For this we are lucky. Thank you all.

The folks at Longfellow Communications had no idea they would become a publishing company, along with their many other talents and public relations savvy. I could not think of anyone I'd rather traverse this unchartered territory than with you—Jess, Clare, Kristin, Rachel, Abby, and Jill. Thank you for your guidance, your diligence, and most importantly, your friendship.

Also, to my editor, the brilliant, bestselling author, Susan Conley. In this role, she has edited what at first had been a mish-mash—she re-structured it in such a way that it came to flow and make sense. She has been a champion of this book from day one. Thank you, Susan, for all you've taught me. I've much more to learn. Onward!

A lot of this book focuses on my work life, all of which really kicked into gear with the inimitable Radio Crew, the original seventeen of us who banded together years ago. Your energy and hard work, your constancy, humor, and your patience got us through those early days—difficult, yes, but we didn't care; we made it fun and ultimately laughed at the situations we found ourselves in. Our early sense of comradery stuck with me and for three decades I'd like to think I carried that with me, sharing it with all the folks I've worked with.

I've had the good fortune of having the best brother and the best sister one could ever have: John and Jackie, thank you for the memories, the grit and the lucky life we've led. Mom and Dad, thank you. Mom, you are gone but you have never left. Dad, thanks for believing in me and being the rock in our lives.

I'd very much like to thank my collaborator, the multi-talented Rose Watson, who took time from her studies of theoretical math to render these amazing illustrations, without which the book would feel incomplete. Rose, I love you—you're the best.

Lastly, I'd like to thank my wife Judy, without whom this book would not have been written. Judy saved my life and she brought me back to life. I was her reclamation project, she, my coach and mentor. I have loved you, Judy, for years. Thank you. I love you.

TW
November 17, 2025
Portland, Maine

www.ingramcontent.com/pod-product-compliance
Ingram Content Group UK Ltd.
Pitfield, Milton Keynes, MK11 3LW, UK
UKHW041903230426
12049UKWH00021B/180/J